BATTLING WITH THE INNER CHILD

BATTLING WITH THE INNER CHILD

JOURNEY TO HOME

Healing My Inner Child to Restore Self-Love

REYHAN TOPLU

ISBN: 978-0-6489542-1-7

#selfpub

www.reyhantoplu.com

To Inner Child In Everyone

CONTENTS

ACKNOWLEDGMENTS

Writing a book is a blessing and more rewarding than I could have ever imagined. None of this would have been possible without my best friend, my sister, Mecexan. You are my true friend, my mentor and supporter. You always stood by me during every struggle, every success and my life journey.Just you know how I love you.

I'm eternally grateful to my dear uncles Shavarsh and Varuj, Sebo, Vasken. I especially would like to thank you uncle Shavarsh I appreciate you always. Your compassion, love, support and respect meant a lot in my journey. You have become a living angel I needed at that time. Thank you all sincerely for having you, your support and presence always.

To my family, my dear parents, brothers, I do not know where I would be if there was not your love and support, and the lessons I learned from you. You believed me no matter what and supported me through everything. I have much love and gratitude for you. Thank you and I am deeply grateful to all my ancestors and my precious grandparents for being part of my life, teaching me and sharing your wisdom all along. I feel so blessed to have you with so much love.

My precious friends Richard, Jenny, Janice, Hisako thank you for cheering me up and supporting me always. My beautiful support team, friends, soul sisters and brothers; Linda ; I want especially thank you dear, glad to have you!, Vange, Helen and Peter thank you for the energy, inspiration and for lifting me up during writing this book. I love you beautiful souls. I truly appreciate you always. Thank you so much for everything.

My dear Gosia thank you so much your precence during my writing and publishing.Thank you my squirrel angel. Much love to you.

I am incredibly grateful to have connected with many amazing people and healers who have supported, inspired and guided me on my journey so far; Cibeli, Mark, Joey, Sharon, Joey, Radhika, Govinda, and the more beautiful whom I have not called your name. I truly thank all of you with deep gratitude.

To my clients and readers, thank you for working with me, trusting and inspiring me, making me laugh and cry right alongside you. I am so grateful to you for being here and I deeply appreciate all of your support.

Finally, as a last word to all those who have been a part of my journey in a visible and invisible way in getting me here, being part of my advancement; people who hurt me, people who loved me, people who taught me happiness and love, people who accept me for who I am, people who embrace me, people who give their compassion, people who inspired me or people who make me feel down, people who uplift me ,people who like me or dislike me, people who make me feel unworthy, people who taught me a life lesson, and people who taught me gratitude and blessings; I am deeply appreciative and grateful for all of your existence past present future....

Thank you. Thank you. Thank you.

REYHAN TOPLU

FOREWORD

By Linda Chiodo

I feel a great deal of honour and blessings to be part of Reyhan's journey, as she brings a delicate and heartfelt piece of work to understand the inner child and guides her audience to self-love.

At the age of 21, I began my adventure on the discovery of self and what I found was the real me. Breaking free of the mind maps designed throughout my childhood and my environment, I embarked on a path to freeing the little girl within to be the woman I am. Today, I live to progress my dreams and can confidently do this due to the healing and the practices Rey shares within these pages.

As a credible and authentic healing practitioner, Rey leads her readers along a beautiful path that helps to untangle the areas in our lives we can often find ourselves stuck in. She sometimes gently and sometimes firmly forces us to face the stories we have created for ourselves that remain in a pain body and do nothing else but hinder our ability to tap into the life we truly desire - filled with abundance and love.

When we bring our consciousness to uncover where we draw our thoughts and emotions from, we can begin to choose the thoughts and feelings that serve us more wisely. For some, this might be from a greater pain place than others. Rey does not discriminate in this way, which is why anyone and everyone will relate to knowing that as children, we all in some way, shape or form carry false burdens due to the underdeveloped reasoning brain and inability to process situations or events rationally.

From diving deeply into our childhood experiences, belief systems, dealing with past hurt, and relationships, Rey brings forth the power of forgiveness, compassion, gratitude and attitude to return the reader to photographs in the childhood mind and refocus the lens to let in more light and love. Rey's writing has you feel that she is beside you, talking you through your own reflections and inner questions to get you to a place where you feel the comfort of home and a sense of inner peace.

The destination you reach by reading this book is yours.Rey gifts her readers with practical strategies that take the wisdom from within to the physical realm.

With such turmoil currently in our external world, Battling With The Inner Child, is a thought provoking yet cozy read that can help soothe the inner turmoil we carry throughout our everyday life experiences.

This book for me, is a reminder of how our limitations are created from childhood and we now have the intellect and power at our fingertips to break beyond our own limitations to appreciate and love ourselves, our lives and our universe.

Thanks, Rey, for taking me, and I am sure many others, on this insightful and nurturing path.

In Gratitude & Love

Linda Chiodo

Leadership and Personal Development - Coach & Facilitator

INTRODUCTION

"The wound is the place where the light enters you."

\- Rumi

What is a paradigm? What is the inner child? There are many words in psychology. Paradigm is one of them. The basic definition is: it is the imaginary lens through which the mind perceives everything and how we see the world. Another way to say is it is your perception and acts according to mind orders. Think of it as a pair of sunglasses through which we see the world. It is a mindset or programming that has control over all habitual behaviors. A paradigm is set up in our minds and we see things via our experience. Many label this as the shadow side, dark side, inner child, or id.

A paradigm has huge influence over perception, the use of time, creativity, effectiveness, logic, productivity, ability to earn money, relationships, all aspects of our lives. When you shift your perception, you unveil yourself from what is outward. The way of doing this is to unlearn, relearn and transform. Where is our paradigm stored? It is a vital question for you because all of our paradigm storage is in our subconscious mind. The subconscious mind is a part of our mind which is shaped by feelings and ıer child is part of the mind (subconscious) being affected while you are a child between conception to 8 years of age. The root is right in the center of your mind. This not the same for everyone. I have noticed that children are particularly affected. Because kid's sensitivity develops quicker than their cognitive reasoning, and then something happens in these formative years with their cognitive reasoning and understanding, their thinking, where one event or a series of events happen between that age gap and creates a strong emotional feeling - a really really overwhelming feeling which traumatizes them. In their logic, catching up with their emotions, triggers very strong emotional reactions. This child is experiencing the feeling but does not have the cognitive reasoning, the thought power, understanding and the knowledge to deal with that feeling. So they are in this position where they going to be believe in their emotions but they do not know how to deal with it. I could say that is the birth of the inner child.

It is a part of your mind that is blocked or stuck in this very important stage. That very part of your mind can not act in a certain way. Every human has those parts of their minds. I can hear you while you say: It must be me! Something is wrong with me! And the child has to deal with this tsunami in his/her mind. And the child vows this for the rest of his/her life. The child believes that vow deeply in his/her core from then on. Even as the child grows right to 60, 70, 80 years of age, he/she believes that because it is still planted in his/her mind. It is frozen and locked in so the inner child sees the world through these spectacles and accepts all these events or experiences he/she held in his/her mind from an immature stage. You act immaturely and you say things that are not true. It is like having somebody there talking in your head. This is how it feels for many. It is your mind, but it is not mature.

Just to give an example to visually understand, imagine you are in a beautiful garden full of flowers, birds, bees and butterflies. Everything is healthy, grooving in harmony, and there is a little patch in the corner, with rubbish and bins. Although seeds lay beneath, they have not germinated because you have to clear all the rubbish away, water the ground, and then the seed will germinate. That is exactly what you have to do in your mind.

Whatever it is called, paradigm or inner child, it is all the same. It is important to ask yourself three questions and speak with your paradigm communication. Ask your inner child what would you like to tell me or what you want. That child suddenly does not know what to say. The inner child will be shocked suddenly. This may be because you need space to talk freely because you may be judged, blamed, abandoned, etc. Communicate genuinely with your inner child in such a way like nurturing your own child. Create space, give time, stop embarrassing, criticizing, being judgmental and comparing your inner child.

Some people misunderstand the inner child. Just because you had your basic needs met as a child, like a roof over your head and food on the table, it does not mean you did not experience early childhood trauma! When I started my inner child healing journey, I asked myself what is that inner child. I could not identify the child within me. I had internal knowledge that a part of me was traumatized and hiding herself from surroundings due to not feeling safe physically and spiritually.

In me, in you and in everyone around you, there is a little child in pain and suffering. There are good times and challenging times. We all experienced those difficulties and most of us experience different levels of traumas in our unique circumstances. This does not mean a small or large amount. When you are in a downswing as a child, you do not know the swing changes to get better. In order to be cognizant of this, you need to use higher mental faculties or laws, but due to the lack of knowledge, experience and surroundings that little child has no ability to manage and ease those traumas. In order to protect and shield ourselves, we try to forget and suppress our subconscious mind from those events, moments or painful times. As a result, we may not be aware of our inner paradigm or inner child even for decades.

The fact that we may ignore or deny and suppress our inner child and send him/her to our rabbit hole (subconscious mind) does not mean the little one is not there. The wounded child is always there, seeking expression and trying to get your attention. While we have many a-ha moments, they are feelings coming to the surface, showing up in our entire life and manifesting as dysfunctional behaviors, habits and experiences. Because that inner child wants to express "See me please! I am here! Help me! Help me! You cannot run away from me." While we hear those inner voices, we want to end our suffering and we try to send the inner child deeper inside as far as possible. It is a pity trying to avoid or run from trauma because it does not help us or end our suffering. We are sending our inner child to the subconscious mind to be frozen not for healing.

The wounded child asks for healing, love and care; but what do we do for that? Do not think of the answer easy. I will tell you now. We do the opposite. We run as much as possible because we do not want more suffering; we are afraid of it. The suffering we experience not only belongs to a moment, but multiple events, and experiences. It can be in any form and does not matter how big or small. It is relative. Those traumas: blocks of pain and suffering in us feels overwhelming. We are not at a certain level of awareness to change our paradigm in that moment. We try to occupy and entertain ourselves within the illusion of our world. That illusion captures us with watching TV. Using the phone, socializing, sex, or using drugs or alcohol. Why all of those? Why do we try those things when we truly we do not want to? Because we do not want to feel that suffering all over again.

The main point here is ignorance because we even do not know the inner child is there. This part of us is reality and in us. Our paradigm is ignorance; the solution is understanding because the ability to see things the way they are, without that lens is freedom for the inner child. But ignorance is inside of each cell of us and our consciousness. This is a like a drop of poison passing throughout our body - organs and consciousness. Ignorance stops us from seeing the source and reality. While we are in that state, we are in an illusion. It gives us pride, false ego, convincing us to make foolish decisions, and it causes even more suffering. The cycle repeats and we go in deeper, closing ourselves from the outside. But in that state, we think there is something wrong with the outside, not the inside of us. Then we try to force to change jobs, relationships, the place we are living, etc. Of course, they may need to change as well, but my point is if change happens in you when your paradigm shifts, your entire life will be changed. You will see everything in a harmonious way. We do not need to go seeking the cause of our suffering outside or far away because it is lying inside of us right now at this moment. The one thing we need to do is look deeply and we can be in touch with that child. How do we touch that child? Everything starts with a thought and that is a seed you need to plant inside of yourself in order to shift and heal your inner child/paradigm. Because our mind is the true source of infinite power and the example of Gandhi has shown that a single individual's strong belief can move whole nations.

When we become aware of a wounded child within us, we feel great compassion for that child and we begin to generate the energy of mindfulness. Because the seed of awakened understanding that supreme intelligence, and happiness is inside of us, we need to turn our spiritual essence. We have a supreme power with which we can communicate and create our reality. We are spiritual beings experiencing a human experience in a human body. So when we came into this incarnation, we forgot why we came here and what powers we are holding. We forgot how to use our higher mental faculties and abilities and then we let the illusion of existence capture us and manifest itself in different forms and names.

One of the main reasons we avoid our inner child is because we are afraid of suffering. This is the subconscious mind where our illusions, programing, paradigm and illusionary beliefs are stored. The mind is a separate self because we suffer from discrimination and delusion. Turn and look at all creatures, animals and every being around you. All have been in their habitat living in harmony. The only creatures living without harmony is human beings and they are living separated from their source. The reason is only human beings have the ability to create their own reality.

CHAPTER ONE

THE INNER CHILD BATTLE

"Happiness does not depend on what you have or who you are. It solely relies on what you think."

- Buddha

Why is our inner child in battle? Why is your inner child almost biting against your adult self and true spiritual nature? How can you end this battle and restore inner peace and harmony?

We are all defining this inner conflict, battle or turmoil. These are uncomfortable and painful red light feelings so the battle manifests itself. It could be anxiety, it could be panic, it could be depression, it could be anger, frustration, hopelessness, or guilt. All of this shows that we know that something is not comfortable inside of us. What is actually happening is what we call the inner child or paradigm. It is an analogy for a part of your mind which is the subconscious mind. This part of your mind is stuck; I would like to define it as the middle of the knot. It is tight and that part of your mind is stuck. When a sensitive child like you, has developed his/ her emotional feelings in advance of their cognitive reasoning or understanding, what I mean by this ,they are creating red light feelings that we could call worry, anxiety, stress, tension, fear or whatever else you want to call it. There are so many names that's why I prefer the term red light because it gives you a definite blanket term. The inner child has developed these red lights but does not understand why and how he/she developed them.

Let's get back to the answer of this question. Why is our inner child in battle? Because the inner child is embracing and countering. Innerchild going through whatever word you want to use, receiving a life lesson from a very challenging situation far ahead of what the little kid can cognitively understand, rationalize and deal with. Now, that could be lots of things. It could be something as serious as abuse, sexually, emotionally or physically. It could also be a disruption in their home life, it could be moving to a new school, or it could be bullying. There is not one worse than the other or better than the other one, so the child goes through this situation where things are not the way the child wants them to be. And here is the deal, the child does not know how to deal with the situation because he/she does not have the knowledge or education, to deal with what's happening. So something happened to the child that he/she does not like, or cannot understand, and if you know this has happened, if you hear yourself saying, "It is not fair. It is not just. It is not the way it should be." This is your inner child or paradigm talking to you. Now you are thinking, "I understand a part of my mind is still immature and it has become stuck, but how is it possible that a tiny little part of our mind can rule our lives and be that powerful to overrule the adult part of us: the more sensible, logical experience possible?" This is part of the armory that the child has to create confusion. The child loves to confuse you, the child part of you loves to put you on the carousel of despair. It is a self-fulfilling prophecy so you have to slow down. This is where meditation, or where I think meditation and focusing your mind, really helps. First of all, remember the child within you encounters the situation that it does not understand. It cannot work out the situation, it does not think it is fair or just, and it is gets stuck. Now, why is it so powerful? This is the why the analogy of the inner child can work because it is almost like you had a physical child and you kept letting that physical child have its own way. If you say bedtime was 9 o'clock and at 9 o'clock the child would not go to bed, and instead cries or shouts, you say "Oh, okay. Stop. You can stay up a little bit later. You can stay up for another hour." You are not giving it what I would call compassionate discipline. I like to make that difference because a lot of people over-discipline. They do not like the word, but if you had a physical child and you let that child run and ruin the house, take over, then the child is not going to listen to you. This is one of the reasons because you have not been listening or compassionately disciplining that part of your mind. That part of your mind slowly, not suddenly; it did not happen overnight but day by day, week by week, month by month, and year by year it has grown and become more and more powerful. That the first little step. You have to give yourself compassionate guidelines and discipline, whatever you want to call it, as criteria that you have to maintain. The second thing that happens when you do not do that, the child gets more powerful, shouts louder and louder, like a naughty and spoiled child. I call it squealing piglets. The child will have a temper tantrum, and if you give in to it, then it just becomes more powerful. I heard an analogy if you give in to a child, it is like throwing red meat at a tiger. It gets stronger and stronger. And if you have been giving in to your inner child, the inner child will get stronger and stronger.What happens instead of seeing this part of your mind as an inner child who is struggling, you see it as some kind of a monster or big problem and you try to shut it out. You do not listen to it, and you do not acknowledge it. It just drives you mad and even I can say from my experience, I said it myself ,"I hate her. She is a monster, she is destroying my life."

Let's get back the question. Why is the inner child seemingly stronger than the spiritual nature (spirit) of you? Your spiritual nature will not step forward, your spirit is your inner knowing, your true self, your higher self, and your inner knowledge. It is like a reference library that's waiting there and I really could not mean it more strongly from this teaching. You are awesome. You have everything you need. That inner knowing and inner strength is there waiting for you, but you get so distracted by this wailing noise and the squealing piglets that you do not go and visit the library of wisdom within. You do not go inside of yourself and find that true knowing that can deal with this inner child because this is not a monster - this a little child. Everyone around us, including yourself, has an inner child. I never found a monster in anyone of us. What I found is a little child who is six, seven, eight, nine or ten years old in the corner scared stiff and terrified. The job is to go and help that part of your mind that I am calling a child because he/she desperately needs help, but the inner child wants to resist as well even if he/she needs help. Imagine if you had a child and every five minutes the child was crying for a chocolate biscuit, and every time he/she cried or had a temper tantrum or became a squealing piglet, you gave in to his/her desires. Over a year or two, you realize the child has become fat and obese, and then child blames you. The inner child part of your mind is exactly like that. It just screams and shouts if you keep giving into it, then gets more and more out of control, eventually, the inner child blames you. And this is when you start saying to yourself, "I am not good enough, I am unlovable, and I cannot cope. You cannot control anything. Everything is too much for you, so you might as well as pack it all in." This is your inner child screaming and shouting. The inner child badly needs spiritual and emotional education and that is the role of an adult. What happens next, When you do not have the answers to give your inner child, listen to your inner child and he/she will say, "I am really concerned about this issue and this is a big problem." As the adult/parent you need to educate the inner child through life lessons, but if you still do not have the answers, where do you get them? Go to your inner reference library, the inner knowledge connecting with the higher self to find answers and find the universal truths. That inner child keeps rejecting these truths. We live in a world of unpredictability and uncertainty; we cannot control external circumstances. Sometimes, people will let us down but it does not mean that people are bad. These are just simple universal truths that the inner child finds so difficult to accept because the inner child always wants to live in Utopia and only wants to get his/her way. As I repeated above, it is up to the adult us to make contact, tap into and connect to our sprit, our inner library and our inner knowledge. You must build yourself, on a rock. Do not build on shifting sand because if you build it on your emotions, you are building your life, who you are and what you represent on shifting sand. It is much better to build on rocks of your spirituality with this inner knowledge. One of the things the inner child is doing is creating the separation and he/she has lost trust in any and everything. It definitely lost trust in you. The biggest misunderstanding is that the inner child is the number one priority. Please listen to me, you are the creator of your emotions. You are not the victim of them. Now, the adult you who is reading this will nod your head and think, "Well, of course, I create my emotions. Of course, they did not float around like a virus and attack me." But I can tell if you were honest.

Secondly, I like to talk about truth, honesty and integrity. After reading this chapter, sit quietly just say; everything in my mind, my thinking, my psyche, my inner thinking, whatever you want to call it, every part (not 99.9%, I am talking about 100%) my innerchild believe that I create 100% of my emotions. If you are honest, there is a little part of you, that part I call the inner child or paradigm who thinks he/she is the victim. When you talk about protection, the need to be safe and secure, because you have built these walls and you cannot trust anybody, this is your inner child. If you start with the words: "I feel unlovable," "I feel this is not fair," "I feel unworthy," "I feel this way, or I feel that way," this is your inner child giving you feelings. You have to replace it with "I think, I believe, and I choose... " and then that teaches your inner child. The first step you are doing is getting yourself in order as an adult because you are addressing the inner child's needs. What I found secretly in the majority of people, including myself, somewhere in your mind you kind of agree with them; when they say, "Oh well, life is really hard. Oh well, I am a victim," and it goes like that and they have a point and you become lost in it because the child goes, "Oh, I am in control now." It is like putting an eight year old in the driver's seat. This is the truth emotionally. I do not care how successful you are in your career, emotionally, you may have an eight year old driving your car. That's the truth so you have to be able to answer these questions.

Now, do you want to know how you can connect with you inner knowing or how you can know if you are connected with your inner wisdom? First, do not lie to yourself. Maybe you think you are not a liar, but I can tell if you do not lie. Everything that goes through your inner voice, that inner talk, has to be the truth. By that, I mean when you tell lies like, "I am not good enough," "I am not lovable," "I cannot cope," or "The world is too much for me," "Everyone is against me," "I am a victim," "Everyone hates me," then you have to give yourself evidence. The cores and the reason, not the result of thinking you are not good enough. You did not come down to the birth canal believing you were unlovable. This is learned behavior, so go back and find out where did you learned it from.

CHAPTER TWO

WHAT ARE CORE BELIEFS ?

"Happiness does not depend on what you have or who you are. It solely relies on what you think."

- Buddha

Core beliefs are basic assumptions about our life in the world that we pick up from when we are very young during our childhood. We get these core beliefs through our parents, our relatives, our peers, our teachers, our culture, from churches, synagogues, mosques we attend. We basically learn from these experiences and develop beliefs about ourselves and how the world works from what people say and how they act.

There are, however, ways in which our beliefs can limit our growth, success, fulfillment, or advancement. As such, if you ask what are some examples of these core beliefs, I am going to give you some examples, but I am going to preface that by saying many of these core beliefs, and matter of fact the majority of them, are negative. Seventy to eighty percent, according to psychologists. Some examples of negative core beliefs are, "I do not deserve love," " I am not worthy," " The world is a dangerous place," "You cannot trust people," "I am not competent," "I am not capable," "I cannot handle things," and more. Those are some core beliefs, the negative ones at least. Why do these beliefs persist and ruin our lives? Before answering this question, we need go back and see how we get them. When our caregivers, when people in the large world are threatening us in a certain way before we are seven years old, we have what Maria Montessori calls an absorbent mind, and the information gets presented to us as children and it comes in directly because we have no filter. It is like a sponge and we absorb it without any questioning or criticism. If a parent is acting negatively or abusively towards us we do not say, "Hey, what is your problem?" We think it is our problem now and we have internalized those things. So as we grow up, the problem starts to repeat over and over towards ourselves. No longer do we need external authority telling us we are no good. We just tell ourselves the same thing so it is constant repetition as we grow older that reinforces the beliefs that we took on when we were younger.

Every unique person has those core beliefs that can lead to being depressed and anxious. In cognitive therapy, we are told that how we think and what we believe affects how we feel and I will give you two examples: one positive and one negative. One of my clients, when she was younger, her mother always used to tell her to watch out and be careful. She was a hyper-vigilant and anxious mother, so from those messages, the child came to believe, "I am not capable and the world is a dangerous place." She repeated those things to herself and really internalized them. By the time she came to me, she was 29 years old, she was living at home and had something called agoraphobia, which means she was afraid of going out into the world and was really struggling to go to school and to find work. In the back of her mind, she kept thinking the world is dangerous and she could not handle things. That is what was keeping her stuck. On the other hand, a man I met at a workshop told me that when he was young, 4 years old, his mother used to whisper in his ear before he went to bed, "You can do anything that you want and there are no limits to what you can achieve." These were really positive messages he absorbed in his subconscious mind, so when he grew up, he was confident. He felt good about himself, he started his own business and he became quite successful. The beautiful thing about this story is now he repeats the same words to his own daughter, giving her the same positive messages that he was given by his parents. This can perpetuate itself to create generations of new and healthy individuals.

There are two ways you can kind of infer your core beliefs. One way is to look around in your world and to see where the negative ones are because that's what we are interested in this chapter, where in your life do you feel stuck, like one person I met in a training course, she said that she was the one always sort of leaving relationships in the first place. Her father had died when she was young and she had this belief that if she got too close to a man, he will abandon her. So if she had this core belief, she was not going to allow herself to get into a significant relationship. The other way is to fill in sentences with your own words. I am ... . People are ... . The world is ...). Fill in the words of those three sentences and notice what you write as word. If it is pessimistic or negative that shows you are carrying some negative assumptions about the world.

There are tools we can use to change these core beliefs and conditionings. The thoughts that we have, the beliefs that we have and restructuring them to eliminate the negative or irrational beliefs, and substitute positive beliefs in their place. For example, I was someone who did not feel competent or capable growing up. That was my conditioning so I started to say to myself, when I started to learn about affirmations, was "I am capable," "I am competent," "I can handle things," "I am resourceful," (that was a big one), "I can attract the help I need," "I have the ability to create support for myself in my life," (that was a really great affirmation I have learned), and "I have the ability to create my reality." That is an example of how you can use affirmations as positive self-talk to reprogram negative beliefs you have taken on from childhood. Maybe at the beginning you did not have the power to determine what they were, but now as a conscious adult, you can choose to believe differently about yourself and about the world. Thereby you can help yourself to heal from the all sources of red light feelings (depression, guilt, shame, and anxiety). If I can do it, you can do it, and everyone can do it.

CHAPTER THREE

CAN I CONTROL EMOTIONAL TRIGGERS?

"These pains you feel are messengers. Listen to them."

- Rumi

Triggers become part of our lives. A lot of people who have been through very harsh and extremely difficult events resonate with them. They are sensitive and aroused. They keep getting triggered by people or situations in their life. Let me explain with an example. You (she/he)say :

"I keep getting triggered by people or situations in my life. I immediately switch on to an emotional high alert mode when people criticize or disrespect me or if I have to deal with any kind of problematic situation at home or work. I am trying my best to keep calm and rise above everything, but actually, I am an emotional wreck and this is wearing me out ... "

When I hear this word this person is doing is taking no responsibility. She is putting the responsibility on something external. She starts from her perspective, "I keep getting triggered." It has nothing to do with what is triggering her. You have to put your finger on your trigger. The trigger is yours, not theirs. Why would you pass over the trigger to them? This is really the most important teaching. Everything here I am mentioning is emotional and personal self-responsibility. Just that first sentence, if she was working with me, I would stop her there and we would do the whole session on the belief system that now forms her entire personality . She has become the victim!?. Yeah, you cannot be the victim of emotions that you create. Remember what I said earlier and repeat it: "I am the creator of my emotions. I am not the victim of them." Other people can't trigger you unless you want to be triggered. Maybe it is sound rough . This is really your path out to emotional freedom. Emotional education is taking control of your life, not trying to control external people to stop ringing your bells or pulling your triggers or whatever I hear every day.

In other words, the other people in those situations, if they are bad situations, they are not to blame for your emotions. There is zero blame on you. If it was not for you, you will say, "I would not feel like that." Well, what you believe is in a vacuum, but we live in a reality. When we hit what I call life lessons, we hit people, unless you want to live in the world with no other people. Would you like that? Everybody would do what you think is right. Everybody would live by your rules. You are the prince or princess and everybody has to follow your rules? That is not the realty that we live in and if you believe that or teach that to your children, you are giving them the completely wrong teaching . The bells, the triggers and the buttons are yours. If we have a front doorbell and I took out the battery, somebody could stand there all day pressing the button and would not know. They could stand there as long as they want. The trigger is something connected to you. It is your responsibility. Do not give up that responsibility, if you do then you have given yourself the wrong end of the stick. Or what I call putting the cart before the horse. You are trying to control them instead of controlling yourself. It's just your ability to be in emotional control, remembering that you create the emotion. If you are experiencing an emotion, you have created it; they have not created it. They have created the event t but how you respond is in your hand .İs not it this more powerful, is not it this more spiritual and is not it this the way that you want to live. You can live by your rules. Do not worry about what other people do. They are busy living by their rules. Why not focus on your rules and live to your belief system?

Lots of people anticipate what a person is going to say or do. The anticipation or the assumption that this situation is going to be really bad allows them to be triggered even by that. It does not mean anything has to actually happen to get an emotional reaction. It is an event or you can call it whatever you want. A situation or a person that is coming into your life, you have to deal with that authentically. This is why I keep saying this is a spiritual matter. This is about honoring and respecting what we call your spirit and your higher self. No one can touch that spirit, except you. When events happen, this is the reality of the world we live in. I am sorry that really bad events have happened to you. Maybe you were made redundant. You lost someone you love, someone you love lost you, families are broken up, you got divorced, you know, everything. This is the reality that we live in. The only thing that you can control is your reaction to that. This is why you do not look outwards; you look inwards. You are in control of you and the major thing, the number one thing, you are the creator of the emotions. Do not let the emotions take over because you are creating it. Then, you are surrendering to the emotions you have just created and you are allowing the emotions to trigger you into being knocked off balance, being pulled onto an emotional high alert and that sense of overwhelm; or we can make a choice to say hold on a minute, I have a total control here. There is no emotional self-responsibility about how I choose to react to this person or to the situation. Or to this thought or anticipation. What you are controlling is you. You are not controlling the situation so that is the key. People try to control the situation instead of controlling themselves, so they react to the situation or person. If we go down the road where we react, blame, become the victim, try to control other people or situations, avoid other people and situations because we do not want to be triggered, it is almost like a human centered mind than sets up a justification for doing it by blaming and saying, "This is not good for me. It was them. It was not me," so we can create a very elaborate justification for holding onto the belief that the problem is external, not absolutely internal. The human centered mind and the inner child is great at blaming other things if it was not for them. If they were just better, "I cannot deal with confrontation." My goodness me! How many times a day do I hear, "I do not like confrontation." THEN DO NOT GET INTO CONFRONTATIONS. It takes two people to have a confrontation. Do not get into a confrontation, learn how to confront. This will take some learning. I do not expect you to do this as you finish this chapter, but I am offering the opportunity to learn and get the support from the community, books and people around you.

You will not get it right the first time. You are not perfect so learn how to confront. How do you learn to confront externally? First, you learn how to confront yourself. You learn how to get your beliefs. You will hear in this book many times, "ask yourself what do you believe and why do you believe it?" That's the key. Make sure your belief system, which involves your emotions, are set on the very firm footing. This makes you actually believe what you are believing. They are lies, they are one of three lies. Keep in mind:"I am not good enough," "I cannot cope," "I am unlovable," make sure it is not one of those. Because those are all lies and if you build the foundations of your belief system on those, your life will be based on those lies. I will guarantee you will experience red light feelings or whatever you choose. If you get those answers, if you get triggered, it is to do with your belief system but equally in some circumstances some people are acting inappropriately and disrespectfully, or some people or situations are horrible. I am not saying that everything is rosy on the outside or everything is perfect in terms of how people around us are and it is all our fault. We are always saying let's just respond in the most authentic way possible. Let's go down this route rather than that route because that route will give you an inauthentic response and an inauthentic reaction. I am saying that we are all sailing on the sea and in this sea there are storms, there are tornados and there are hurricanes. There are whales and octopuses in this sea, and we have to deal with them appropriately; when the storm comes, we do not open the sails. We keep ourselves quiet. We find a way through and that is your responsibility. That is not the responsibility of the storm. The storm did not come your way and there are tremendously dysfunctional people and events that happen, which are not right, fair or just and you take responsibility for how you respond. I want you to be more proactive than the reactive. I am saying here, you instead of being reactive you need to be responsive. And to not go down this old familiar path where you say, "I am the victim," "I am being triggered," "If it was not for them, I cannot live my life," or "No wonder I am an emotional wreck." You know, this has to stop because you are awesome. Why not take responsibility for your emotion and you have everything you need. This is spiritual teaching. Your essence is perfect. There is nothing that you need. You have everything. What I am saying is to look within, open that storage door and get everything you have in that respect.

These situations and people are almost here to teach us a lesson to signpost us. If we have an extreme emotional reaction, what we call a red light feeling, that person or situation that teaches us about that personal situation is like a spiritual signpost to a life lesson that needs to be learned. For example, if I get triggered, if I have red light feeling, if someone disrespects me or does not validate me when I believe I should be validated, I guess they will empowering the lie to in my belief system that I am not lovable. That is the number one lie and a lot of people can just say this is the way others disrespect them. Whether it is someone at work or someone close to us, a friend or a partner, they could ignore or criticize us and that will trigger a kind of inauthentic belief within us that we are not lovable and then we blame that person. We blame that situation and we do not look within us. Do you ever look at that person when you are experiencing those red light feelings? Why not look at the person and ask, "Should I put value on what they say?," "Are they somehow totally balanced?," "Are they superior to me?," "Are they emotionally or intellectually superior to me?," and "Is what they say about me the truth?" Of course, not because most people you meet anyway have a mask up and what you see is not what is going on inside them. Do you think that you are the only one with the inner child? Everybody has them. I have them, you have them, everyone around has them inside. We all have this part of our mind trying to rub you with whatever is stocked inside. There is nobody immune to this. Do not think anyone is. Do not think that you are the only one that is experiencing these thoughts. This is what I am explaining to you, clarifying these thoughts and get it clear.

Dear problem, thank you for coming into my life. There must be something here I have to a learn because until I learn that lesson, guess what? It will keep coming around. How many times has this happened to you? Different people, different events, but the same problem. And that is because you have never learned and here is the wonderful teaching: once you have solved the problem, you can never have it again. It goes away and never returns. If it keeps returning, all it is telling you, you have not solved the problem. Do not look externally, look internally.

Whether it is a friend or family or a situation at work, it can be the same inauthentic lie that is being tweaked, being scratched like an itch. You have something scratching the itch. The fact is you have the lies. So, the lie that "I am unlovable or not good enough" could be scratched because someone treats you in a disrespectful way or ignores you. You believe you are not being validated or you believe that you are not needed or you surplus to requirements all sorts of in these situations. People can trigger you or they can scratch that itch but it is yours. It is your itch that you need to look at and resolve, and then it does not matter what people do because it is still not great if someone disrespects you or abuses you, but at least it does not affect your internal world so badly if somebody disrespects you. For me, that would say more about them. I would look at them and think, "You have some emotional issues here. It has nothing to do with me," because I am not looking for your respect. To be honest, I would allow and I accept that they can respect or not respect me, and that's their choice because, you know what? I respect me. There is the key. I respect me and I do not need the stamp of validation from someone else. If you are looking for that stamp, you are looking around all the time for this validation, for this approval, and that's when you start pleasing people and trying to not upset them. You are always looking for something from them. It is like you are needy and you want it. You have to have it. You have to have that reassurance. You have to know what is certain; you want to know the future; you want to know what is going to happen. The truth is we do not and I am not going to accept that. We have a problem because that is the reality.

If someone disrespects you, and if we do not hold the lie that we are not good enough or we are unlovable, then it is not going to upset our internal emotional balance so much. Also, we are more likely, if we go down this road to put in place authentic and appropriate boundaries and to be able to speak our truth and say this is not appropriate. But if we play this blame game and become the victim where it is them and not me, then we do not have the authentic ability to put in place and speak those boundaries to people.

If you have red light feelings such as blame, shame, anxiety, anger, etc. and you have these feelings where you do not have the control of the situation or a situation is not predictable or a situation is uncertain, so you experience red light feelings whether it is anxiousness or overwhelming feelings .And then you want to close yourself in. That again relates to the belief in the lie, the core belief that, "I cannot manage, I cannot cope," so that's the third lie I mentioned. "I cannot cope," is wanting to be certain that you are going to be with me for the rest of my life, and the truth is, we cannot be certain. You may change your mind, you may not want to be with them for the rest of your life, but nobody can give you that certainty. When it is someone taking responsibility for their emotions, they want that certainty because they do not want to experience the emotion. They are looking at the wrong place. Instead of that, l want you to control the emotions. Of course, we do not want people to leave us, but we cannot control that so someone can choose not to be in your life. But they cannot reject you because that is you being the victim again. You are not the victim. You are a spiritual, wonderful, divine and awesome human being. How can you be a victim to someone else? They are not superior and you are not inferior. You do not put them on the pedestal. This is the wrong belief system, so this goes to the core beliefs. You have to ask yourself. Why do you think that affects you? Why? Why? Why? You will come down normally to three lies I have mentioned previous pages which are I am not lovable, I cannot cope, I am not worthy.

Also, there is an extreme reaction for these emotional triggers and what people call PTSD (Post-traumatic stress disorder) or some form of trauma. Obviously, a lot of PTSD can be from adult experiences, but trauma also can be related to childhood experiences, traumatic experiences, or abuse. What I want to say here is the same process, same issues in terms of as an adult in our everyday life, there are certain people, situations or things we believe that are going to happen. That triggers a rankle (cause of continues annoyance) that affects or scratches these inauthentic beliefs within us. In other words, this means we have unresolved issues, what I call life lessons. Something that has happened to you earlier in your life, normally childhood, and you did not have the cognitive awareness or the ability to deal with it then, you have created the red light feelings without realizing you are creating them. That's what I am trying to remind you. I know the intellectual side of you reading this book will say, "Yes, I agree with you, Rey. Of course, I create my emotional feelings," but ask that part of your mind which we call the inner child and that part of your mind quiet during meditation, "My darling, do you believe that you create the red light feelings?" I will almost guarantee you, it does not. It believes the red light feelings are coming externally - coming into it like an attack. That's why you have to use words like triggered; "I am triggered." I would prefer you say "I choose to be triggered." People hate when I say that because they do not want to take responsibility. They want to say these emotions are flooding in and, "Reyhan, and I cannot do anything about it, except protect myself." This is where it goes wrong because you build a wall of protection, but you are keeping the who you are within you. You are building a prison and locking yourself in. The adult part of yourself may know rationally that you have control over your inner world if you choose to take it. However, that part of our mind that we call the inner child can be so loud, can be so determined and can go in a fight or flight mode. It wants to run away from what it perceives is a very bad situation, abusive situation, or disrespectful situation. It wants to lock itself in so it is so high or it wants to scream and shout that this is not fair or how this person is treating me unfairly.

This situation is like it is not fair so it feels almost like we are being pulled apart. Then you say the child goes into a lockdown mode and gets very stubborn because it wants to keep itself safe and protected. What all that means is that almost depends on you how to resolve . And you dig your head in the mud and say "You know it is them and not me" and you do not put in the work. That's why the metaphor of being in a child, though not perfect of course, it is an excellent metaphor because that part of your mind that is the inner child. This inner child is the most willful, strongminded, and my goodness can he/she scream loudly! It is very challenging and it is one of the greatest spiritual journeys that you will embark on to bring the inner child in you into a oneness. This is why all of these are spiritual teachings because you are one. You are awesome. You are not separate. You are not fighting each other. You a=re not in a tug of war with that inner critic. You know who that is: that's you talking to you. You would not talk to other people the way you talk to you. I am missing when I say first step ; stoooop , stop it. stop it! Do not beat around the bush. Do not go and say "Let's talk about it 2 year later, no stop it! and please ask 3 vital questions; and find out why you are doing it ?

So that normally involves us taking some responsibility in that moment. We pause or stop it. We do not go down the normal road of being dragged down to the extreme emotional reactions like shouting and screaming or withdrawing. We say, "Hold on, what is going on here?" Let's look at the beliefs you have. Let's look at the lies we are holding onto. What we are thinking here? What are we believing here? We take it down level by level, from red light feelings to the thoughts and self-talk, down to the core beliefs and we may find that we ask the questions, "What am I thinking? What am I believing? Is this the truth?" We get down to that original experience or series of experiences. Whether it was something traumatic that happened to us in adulthood or more often than not, something that we have to imagine happened to us in childhood that we did not understand or we could not make sense of. We need to unlock what we need to resolve because that event or series of events that we misunderstood which made us first go into lockdown in an extreme reaction because that is what is forming our emotional reactions as an adult today.

So the point is I cannot change your belief system. No one can because it is your belief system, but when we find the life lesson, the unresolved issue if you prefer, then we can widen the beam and we can look at other possibilities and other ways of viewing it by offering different perspectives of that situation. We cannot change the situation because it happened 10, 20, 30, 40 or 50 years ago. We are not trying to change the situation. We are also not trying to forget the situation. That's the last thing we are trying to do. What I am trying to say is take control of your perceptive, your beliefs and your thinking around that situation. That is really the most important thing because, in my experience, I am so fortunate to deal with absolutely amazing people. I learned lots of life lessons from them. All those people are very successful, you know, really doing well on the paths that form their lives. But emotionally, I am sorry they have a 6, 7 or 8 year olds at the front of the car, driving the car, and they do not know how to deal with that. Once upon time, I was one of those people. This is when they use triggers, and then they start eating too much, drinking too much, hiding away and not going out, putting themselves down, and whatever else. Instead of being proactive in their life, they are reactive to the emotions they create. And that's the breakthrough for me. Every part of you, 100%, not 99%. Oh, I am with you 99%. I say, "No, no sorry. Let's work 100%." You have created every emotion you have experienced .

Once you have done that inner work, it can be so releasing, so transformative, and then it is like it deeply grounds you into your authentic self so that you can then tackle the situation, the person or whatever is knocking you off balance. Now, you are more strongly rooted and you can go to deal with that person or situation with confidence, authenticity, clarity and focus. This is what I mean by effortless effort, being in your flow like walking a tightrope. You see in places where people walk a tightrope high in the mountains, when you go home you think, "Oh my goodness! I would not be able to do that because the rope starts swinging." Well, that is life - we are walking this tightrope. You have to learn how to walk, how to balance and how to be in your flow to create effortless effort. It does not matter whether the people you meet are dysfunctional or highly functional because you are in your flow and you do not let them knock you off your tightrope. You are walking your turn. You are a tightrope expert, and it does not matter whether the tightrope goes in a circle, you will be able to adjust. I have never surfed, but I am sure when I watch others surf, you are going to ride the wave and you cannot stop the wave. You have to learn how to ride the wave. I will go a bit further; it is almost like when you get yourself into that position, you welcome the next big wave because it allows you to hone your skills, to be authentically responsive, to be able to transform the situation, to flow with situations and to adapt with situations. From that, you can reach your true potential and you will occasionally fall of your board as well, but what do you do? Get back on again. That's what you do because you will not surf every wave and that's what life is like. This is something really exciting. This is who you are as a spiritual person. This is the reality you live in. This is the wonderful life you are so blessed to have. Look at your skin, look at your fingers, look at your eyes and everything around you in detail. This is amazing. This is your life. It is amazing that you are even here. It is even more amazing that you are reading this book. And we are everywhere in the world, we get connected. Is this not -amazing? This is how blessed you are. Do not deny your blessings, surf those waves if you like the analogy.

It was in 1994 that Antonio Damasio a neuroscientist published his book Descartes Error and here is what he says, when he is talking about learning, he used to assume learning cognition intellectualization was a separate entity in a separate process from emotionality. You know, Homo sapiens is the Latin name of our species. The man knows so we are assuming this is an intellectual definition of humanness, but what Damasio said in his work is cognition is actually something that rests on an edifice of emotion so that basis of learning and cognition is actually our emotional being. That emotional being very much connected to our visceral states in the states in our liver, stomach, heart, lungs and all our internal organs. The mind itself and the brain itself is an organizational entity that brings together information coming to it from the outside and inside at the same time. In fact, the brain receives more messages from the inside of the body than sometimes from the outside. The messages it receives from the inside has a lot to do with how well we can engage with the external world. That means the capacity to pay attention and to learn has a lot with what is happening internally on the visceral and emotional level. What our gut feelings are telling us, so in a society where people are less than less connected their gut feeling, there is a less and less engagement with the realities of the external world and their gut feelings. Even though we are externally focused in a less efficient manner because of this disconnect. And tell me, did you have an experience of a strong gut feeling about something, ignoring it and being sorry or glad afterwards? I am sure you had one or maybe more. It is absolutely valid, and we ignore it at our peril, but that's a function of living in a society that actually cuts us off from our gut feelings. There is something internal that knows that is much stronger than what the intellect is telling us in any contest between the internal knowledge and the intellectual knowledge. Ninety-nine percent of the time that internal knowing will be accurate and the intellectual rationalization will be inaccurate. Damasio says the lower levels in the neural edifice of reason is the same one that regulate the processing of emotion and feelings along with the body functions necessary for the organism's survival. This is calling us to have a view of knowledge, learning and cognition that takes into account emotionality and our internal body fades.

"In turn, these lower levels maintain direct and mutual relationships with virtually every bodily organ, thus placing in the body directly within the chain of the operations that generate the highest reaches of reasoning, decision making, and, by extension, social behavior and creativity" Damasio states.

Let me give you an example of a situation. We have millions of children being diagnosed because of their behaviors and those millions of children are getting stimulant medications, controlling their behaviors and conditions. What I have here is a massive social experiment on the chemical control of children's' brains because we do not know what else to do. When children do not learn the way we want them to or say sorry the way we expect them to, and they do not behave the way we expect them to, we have two dominant responses. One response is to medicalize it. Let's call it a medical name and let's medicate it. I am talking about the overwhelming domination of the pharmacological approaches to childhood issues, inner child issues. There is that response, medical approach, and there is the biggest behavioral approach. The behavioral approach is saying here is what is wrong with the behavior itself, so let's control the behavior and that, sadly, dominates psychology these days. So, the problem is the behavior when your inner child acts out. Let's control the behavior. Parenting books will tell you when this is happening; this is what parents should do. The child acts out and parents should have some way of managing that behavior. Here is the thing about acting out, look at the phrase itself. It is a good English phrase. It is a very specific meaning. We act out and it does not mean we are behaving badly. We act out when we do not have the language to say something in words. That's what acting out actually means. If you landed in a country where nobody spoke your language and you had to portray hunger, you have to act out. Kids are acting out all the time. We all act out all the time in different forms. Our response is to control the behavior, we respond to the form of the message rather than to the contents of it, and then we wonder why dos not work. İn Sydney, a school, one year ago I think, there was 8 or 9 years old boy who end up in handcuffs because the cops were called and then this kid had an Asperger's. This diagnosis which involves poor social processing and poor impulse control, among other features, and this kid had been bullied. He was very upset, he was screaming and the teachers who were there decided he needed to be isolated. How often we do that to kids? We isolate them. Well, he was put in a room by himself at which point he really freaked out and neurophysiologically he needed something very different, and I will come to that later. When they were isolating him, he started throwing things and I think destroying the furniture, and that's why they called the police who handcuffed this nine year old. The debate afterwards was, "Oh, was the police right to do this to the kid?" But that was not the right question. When you call police, they are going to do what police do, which is to restrain. That's what they are trained to do. The real question was how come well-meaning, and I assume all educated teachers in a major school system are, had no understanding that what the child needed at that moment was emotional closeness with a nurturing adult to regulate his neurophysiology that so needed at that moment .And these incidents are not totally isolated. I mean, handcuffing is isolated. Take an example from my childhood. One of my neighbors, a lady, because her child was hyperactive, in order to control her child's hyperactivity, she taped her child's hands and legs. This is how she learned to control his hyperactivity. Another way to understand all of what I am saying, these behaviors rest on emotional standards and expectations and do not serve the child. We have to ask ourselves what was happening with that child emotionally in that moment, and let's face it, we all have and are still experiencing those emotional ups and downs, all circling around the inner child, beliefs, and paradigms. There are more kids having behavioral problems, impulse regulation problems, body regulation problems, emotional outbursts, difficulties with learning, and this is burgeoning in our society. But my question is, why is this so? Is it because of some genetic disease? Is someone mysteriously spreading it in the population? Or something is happening in children's lives that is undermining their capacity to socially interact well, to pay heed, to pay attention, to be emotionally regulated, to have impulse regulation, and to be able to regulate their inner turmoil. I am sure you have been hearing what the brain is today; the prefrontal cortex has nine very important functions. It regulates the body itself. The prefrontal cortex is the mammalian cortex, the one that's the latest to develop, evolutionary speaking, and it really is what distinguishes us from other creatures. The prefrontal cortex directly in our forehead, it regulates the body, it regulates attune communications with others, it is responsible for emotional balance, it provides insight, it provides empathy, it modulates fear so if something happens, the fear circuits, brain will take over the prefrontal cortex to override that fear circuit saying, "Okay, calm down. You can actually handle this."

The prefrontal cortex allows us respond with flexibility. This means if you say something to me that might upset me, instead of reacting by screaming back at you, I can actually say, "Oh okay, what's happening with you? Why did you say that to me? Do I really take it personally?" And then, I can respond rather than react. The prefrontal cortex also regulates intuition and morality. These nine functions of the cortex are actually supported by mindful awareness practices, seven of them, at least. Here is the key, they are supported and developed by nurturing parenting. I think all nine of them are because what we are actually coming down to, in our society and the reason so many children are facing so much inner turmoil, is because the parenting environment has become so stressed where parents are no longer able to provide their children with the environment that these functions and prefrontal circuits needed to serve these functions and can develop properly. That's why this is an- epidemic. It is not only bad parenting, it is not only drinking water, it is not only some genetic disease that is spreading. What is going on is that conditions for healthy brain development of the prefrontal cortex is less and less available for children. The thing is young human beings have to develop an adaptive mechanism to survive early traumas. If I stress to you right now by threatening you or just insulting you, insulting your dignity as a human being, you would have three healthy options: you can walk out and escape and the other would be to fight or challenge by standing up for yourself; and if for whatever reason you are unable to engage in either of those modalities, you have the third option; you could not read this book, put it aside, in person you could seek help and you can say this person is bugging me. If none of those are available to you and the stress was immense and intense, your brain would escape from that. Escaping would be to just disassociate, to tune out, so tuning out is not a disease, it is a nature-given capacity that we have to escape overwhelming inner turmoil. What I did not know was found out almost by accident. It was the human brain itself, the very circuits in the prefrontal cortex that I have mentioned, both of those functions develop under the impact of the environment, so that which circuits develop, which prefrontal circuits develop, and how the emotional circuits develop, depends very much on the early environment in the childhood. An example is that of vision. If you do not see light five years after birth, it does not matter how good your eyes are or how good your genes are, you will be blind for the rest of your life because it takes light waves to promote the development of the visual circuits. It is that simple with the emotional self-regulation circuits that are not functioning very well in our kids these days, with the attentional circuits that are not functioning very well, with the impulse regulation circuits and with the stress regulation circuits. It is the same thing, just like light is needed for vision, the right environment is needed. For those circuits to develop, I am talking about physiological development, I am talking about the neurochemistry of the brain, I am talking about oxytocin, serotonin, dopamine, endorphins and all the important neurochemicals that modulate our behaviors. The quantities of their interaction with the surface that modulates them. They depend on environment for their development and the human brain is particularly vulnerable because, unlike other animals, most of our brain development occurs after birth. We also know what happens during pregnancy has a significant impact on the developing brain of the child, so the more stressed women are, the more likely the kids are going to be more affected. If you are looking at the preponderance of autism, and all other kinds of childhood conditions, we are looking at the impact of inner turmoil or stress on the parenting environment, including pregnant women. A study conducted after 9/11 looked at the stress hormone levels of one year old infants whose parents, mothers, had suffered post-traumatic stress disorder as a result of 9/11 (twin tower attack) during pregnancy. These children at one year old had enormous stress hormone levels which means that their stress regulation circuitry had been negatively affected by the mothers' stress during the pregnancy. This means they are more prone to addictions, behavioral problems, and learning difficulties because too much cortisol, the stress hormone interferes with learning and actually shrinks the hippocampus, which is the part of the brain responsible for retaining memory. One could speak to you for at least ten hours a day just on the effects of the parental stress. There was another study in 2012 where they looked at genetic functioning. We have this whole idea that genes regulate things and that genetics control things. They do not. Genes are turned on and off by the environment. That study is called epigenetics. Epigenetics is how genes are regulated by the environment, so that in both human studies and animal studies, we know that even if people have certain genes that might predispose them to addictions, if they are brought up in nurturing environments those genes are turned off. This study also showed 90 percent of teenagers had been affected by stress on the mother in the early years of life. Ten percent of kids had been affected by stress on father in the preschool years, so the stress on the parents translate into the genetic expression of the teenagers a decade later so the environment actually modulates the activity of genes.

The architecture of the brain constructed is an ongoing process that begins before birth, continues into adulthood and establishes either a fragile foundation for all health learning and behaviors that follow. Then, the interaction of genes and experiences literally shapes the circuitry of the developing brain and it is critically influenced by mutual responsiveness of the adult-child relationships, particularly the early childhood years. The key issue is the mutual responsiveness of adult-child relationships that is a spectrum. On one hand, you can have the calm non-depressed emotionally present attuned parent, and on the other, you can have the parent who abuses the child, traumatizing the child. I have been working with kids and adult for long years and I did not have a single kid or teenager or adult who was not sexually, physically, mentally or emotionally abused as a child. In between is that calm attuned non-stressed spending environment, which is what people offer themselves when they practice mindful awareness. It works in between the extremes, the modalities, of parents who actually act out their own traumas on their children by traumatizing them. There is a whole range in our society that increasingly moving towards stress because parents no longer have the support they used to have long ago with the extended family, tribes and villages. There was an article at Notre Dame University long times ago and they looked at the optimal parenting environment; it was the hunter-gatherer tribe because the hunter-gatherer tribe parents were present physically with their kid Multiple adults of multiple generations will connect emotionally with kids. The parents were always with the kids and so on and so forth. The more time spent has nothing do with bad parenting. It has to do with stress parenting and when the parents are stressed, they are less able to attune to their kids which makes it more likely that their children's brain will not develop optimally. That is what educators are up against these days.

When I looked further at what the impact of early traumas are on the child's brain and the capacity to learn, where we up against those coping mechanisms, but the child adapted (accepted as beliefs), and one coping mechanism was disassociation, the tuning out. The problem is when the child has accepted those core beliefs chronically, in early childhood that is programmed in the part of the mind which I called the inner child. For example, ten years later, when Lia is 55 years old, she is diagnosed with ADHD. There are times in the first year of life when every second, consider this carefully, millions of circuits are being laid down and millions of connections are being made. It is that rapid. It is that intense. The brain grows, so if inner turmoil happens in the parent's life during that period, for example, if the mother is depressed after the parents have separated, one parent left the other, the father is overworked, or there are unresolved family issues that will have an impact on a child. I am not talking about learned behavior here, I am talking about emotionally based coping mechanisms. Now, that's one way the inner child protects itself from trauma or stress. Another way the inner child protects itself from stress is an emotional shutdown by not being aware of feelings. Incidentally, when you put your hand up and say you had an experience of a gut feeling and ignoring it, you were telling the story of your childhood, do you know that? And this story was your authentic emotions were not responded to by your parents, not because they did not love you, but because they were too stressed and traumatized. That means you disconnected because it was too painful that your feelings were not validated by the world, you learned to disassociate your gut feelings from your intellect, and then you became stupid in the sense of the inner knowing no longer being available to you. Now at the extreme case of that, you have people who totally shut down emotionally. The problem with shutting down emotionally is you stop learning! Emotional learning stops when you shut down because you shutdown to protect yourself, but for development you need vulnerability. Vulnerability comes from the Latin word vulnery, which means "to wound," so our vulnerabilities are our capacity to be wounded. Nothing grows when you are not vulnerable. A tree does not grow when it is hard and thick. It grows when it is soft, green and vulnerable. It is the same with children. When they shut down emotionally, they have difficulty in learning, especially from the negative experience so they keep repeating the same stuff over and over again. Despite the negative consequences, they learn nothing from it, then the adult gets exasperated, "I told him a thousand times not to do this and he is still doing it." Well, the proper response is if you have told him a thousand times, and he is still doing it, who has the learning problem here? Clearly, what we have to do is find out what is going on with that child. The third way of emotional sub protection is detachment from relationships and particularly from relationships that threaten you, so a lot of kids are detached from adult relationships and by default, as I pointed out, learning also stops because for the learning you need curiosity, but curiosity is vulnerability. When you are curious, you care about something. When you emotionally shutdown, you do not care about anything. Everything is boring and does not matter.

Number one also you learn from trial and error; this requires vulnerability because you have to admit something does not work and be sad about it. When you defend it against sadness because nothing matters you are not going to learn from negative experiences. You are not going to try something again, instead, you can say, "I do not care," and you just give up. I do not care about the frustrated child; people learn through attachment. In other words, when you are emotionally attached to somebody, you want to emulate that person. You want to be like that. You want to learn from that person. Well, that's fine in societies where children still are attached to adults, but what happens in the society when children are emotionally connected to each other so much so that they cannot bear to be without each other for one moment. Every second they are not physically in each other's presence, they have to be texting one another. That's not a technological problem. It is an attachment problem. It also means that they are not learning from the adult who actually tells them what life is about. They are learning from immature creatures, so these are the consequences of those early adaptive mechanisms on learning.

This is required for the learning capacity of young human beings to really express themselves before recording in the part of brain as an inner child. The human being has three fundamental ways to respond to the environment and these follow an evolutionary ladder, if you will. Our fundamental mode, or at least, I should say, our most primitive mode, is the reptilian one. The reptilian brain is our brainstem down low in the brain and we share this with reptiles. The reptiles are creatures that are cold blooded and they cannot expand a lot of energy. They have to conserve energy. Their method of doing this mental challenge is to freeze and sink under the water so they do not have to use too much oxygen, conserving their energy. That's the function of certain brain circuits which, when activated, will put us into a freeze mode. This is fine for the reptile, but it can be deadly for a human being and it certainly interferes with learning. The second mode is the mammalian flight-fight response which happens higher up in the brain. It activates the sympathetic nervous system, allowing the so-called flight-or-fight response which involves adrenaline and cortisol, the stress hormones, to give us more sugar. This is a bit more energy which increases our heart rate so we have more blood pumping to our brain and our muscles and so on. This is all fine, but the problem is that these are both defensive modes, and the human organism can either be in a defensive mode, or a growth mode or learning mode, but not both at the same time. The mode in which we are in, the learning phase, is when I am paying attention to another person, when I am listening to the message that they are delivering, when my middle ear muscles are activated in such a way as to take in verbal information, when my head turns towards someone so I can observe that person's face and respond to his/her facial expressions, and when I am taking in and responding to the prosody and modulation of his/her voice. That is yet another brain circuit and it activates a totally different set of nerves in addition to part of the nervous system, and that's called the social engagement mode. The nerves that regulate our social engagement behavior are very much connected to the nerves that carry information from our viscera, our internal organs, and the nerves that, simultaneously, regulate our breathing to make it shallow or deep. That is our social engagement mode, but to be in this mode, we have to feel safe. We have to feel emotionally safe. Now, let me say something, as a researcher and educator interested in ADHD and inner child traumas, how many adults in their 30s, 40s and 50s I come across, people who speak with choked tones and sometimes tears in their eyes about something that a teacher or parent said to them decades ago that was humiliating. The teacher or parent meant nothing harmful or may have been aware of it, they might have been trying to humorously support the kid, but as recent research shows, there seems to be receptors in our temporal lobe that relate to our degree of safety, emotional safety, and when we do not feel safe or feel fearful, the fight-or-flight mechanisms are engaged. When the child is not engaged in the fight-or-flight mechanism, they cannot learn. When we yell at a child, exclude, isolate, them when we look at him/her harshly, use a tone of voice that expresses our irritation and lack of comprehension, when we do not understand the child's emotional state; so the child feels like they are opposing us. We are actually triggering the defensive state. One of the things that mindfulness practices teach kids is to regulate their internal states. But surely, as long as they are immature and given that they are so connected to the adult, children are necessarily dependent on the environment because they are not independent. They are not mature as long as that's the case and, incidentally, this is the truth for a lifetime as their emotional states, their visual states, their heart and lungs, their nerves' receptivity, and their sense of safety, depends purely on the environment. It is up to us to provide that emotional safety for them, and that's much more important than academic learning. I am trying to convey, not that is not important, but without that emotional basis to it, to just will not penetrate. When fear is removed, it is empowering. If your nervous system is safe, you can do lots of interesting things. When your nervous system detects risk and fear, you cannot even sit in your room without being hypervigilant, and that depends very much on our internal perception of safety. Now, the problem is when children grow up in dysfunctional environments, it is increasing that they do, they do not even perceive safety when it is there. They mistake safety for a lack of safety and, unfortunately, they sometimes mistake a lack of safety for safety. These are the kids who are getting into trouble. Our jobs as educators, parents, or anybody who has anything to do whatsoever with children, is primarily and first of all, is not to forget about childhood traumas, but to prioritize them. The first priority has to be the absolute emotional security of our children.

CHAPTER FOUR

DYSFUNCTIONAL FAMILY ENVIRONMENT

"Do not feel lonely, the entire universe is inside you."

- Rumi

There are many things shaping our inner child. I would like to start with one of powerful element in our life: our family environment and culture. Basically, whatever goes on around us, we accept, put in a fixed format and place it in our subconscious mind. This is the reason why most traumas happen in a dysfunctional family. What is a dysfunctional family?.

A dysfunctional family is a family in which conflict, misbehavior, and often child neglect or abuse on the part of individual parents occur continuously and regularly, leading other members to accommodate such actions. Children sometimes grow up in such families with the understanding these situations are normal. Dysfunctional families are primarily a result of two adults, one typically overtly abusive and the other codependent, and may also be affected by addictions (such as substance abuse e.g. drugs, including alcohol), or sometimes by an untreated mental illness. Dysfunctional parents may emulate or overcorrect from their own dysfunctional parents. In some cases, the dominant parent will abuse or neglect their children and the other parent will not object, misleading a child to assume blame.

Some features are common to most dysfunctional families:

Lack of empathy, understanding, and sensitivity towards certain family members, while expressing extreme empathy towards one or more members who have real or perceived "special needs". In other words, one family member continuously receives far more than they deserve, while another is marginalized.

Denial which is the refusal to acknowledge abusive behavior, possibly believing that the situation is normal or even beneficial.

Inadequate or missing boundaries for self (tolerating inappropriate treatment from others, failing to express what is acceptable and unacceptable treatment, and tolerating physical, emotional or sexual abuse.)

Disrespect of others' boundaries (physical contact that another person dislikes, breaking important promises without just cause, and purposefully violating a boundary another person has expressed.)

Extremes in conflict (either too much fighting or insufficient peaceful arguing between family members.)

Unequal or unfair treatment of one or more family members due to their birth order, gender, age, family role (mother, etc.), abilities, race, caste, etc. This may include frequent appeasement of one member at the expense of others, or an uneven/inconsistent enforcement of rules.

All of us have been a child, experiencing intense emotions, which are red light feelings, you need to look at them. They blocked you; we should never underestimate them because they really are powerful experiences. It is totally understandable to try to protect and control feelings as much as the child does due to his/her cognitive reasoning being undeveloped, he/she can act in a certain way that creates a new negative experience. I just need to point this out, part inner child is they do not realize they create emotional experience. What do I mean by this ? This means they are not creating an external environment, they are not creating the experience of someone abusing them or someone leaving the family home they loved most. I am not talking about that stuff. They are creating negative thoughts and negative feelings. They are creating red light feelings and emotional experiences in response to an external situation which could be a tough and challenging event or series of events to verbalize. But they don't have and learned knowledge and life lessons to address that situation. This can be really extreme situations like a death in the family, divorce in the family or moving away from home. For adults, those things are not important, but changing schools, having anew child come into the family, being bullied, or something as simple as not getting a good result from a football team or basketball team. They do not know how to deal with these emotional experiences inside of the body, but, instead of understanding they have created them, they believe these have come from outside, almost attacking them. They build a defense to protect themselves. We do not know how it works. We do not know acting in a certain way causes this. This is the basic explanation of the cycle of the inner paradigm.

When the kid reaches a certain age, they have to take responsibility to change, but it is really very important to point out that the inner paradigm stayed at the age he/she experienced the trauma, emotion, event or situation. While you grow the paradigm, the inner child, stayed at that level and did not grow. So I believe, while you read this, you can think about yourself now in a moment, and do you agree with what you think, what you say, what you believe you are experiencing that way? The degree of understanding and taking responsibility for the way we are feeling will change everything radically. You just need to take leap of faith and follow it.

Your childhood does not define you and set up the rest of your life. It cannot. This very important. Please repeat this to yourself three times because I want you to take full emotional and personal self-responsibility. I want you put your hand on the wheel. I want you to drive your Ferrari. I do not want you to be sitting in the back seat and telling others how they should be driving your car. This is what happens when this immense event happens. This massive event in our life in our childhood happens and, believe me, it happens to all of us, not only you! You are not victim. you need to cognize this first. That's proof to me of how awesome you are, to be able to travel through that part of your journey. This is your journey, if you are reading this, you may now understand all the things you experienced in childhood, does not define you. You can now take responsibility and you cannot change what you do not understand, so you have to go back to look at your core values ,thinking and beliefs that were keeping you trapped in this paradigm. You stay and live you're your paradigm or inner child if you are not going back to explore it. I love this quote, though I do not know where it is from, "Exploration is power judgement is weakness." Do not judge. I am not telling you to accept or reject it, just explore it and you will find the truth about yourself and your paradigm.

When you are driven by your inner child, you are still working with the belief system of a child between the ages of one to eight years old. This is why this does not work for many, whatever they try. You have to update your belief system, shift your paradigm because the child within is carrying faulty acquisitions and faulty beliefs into adulthood. It affects all environments and relationships, and then, your inner child says, "I am right," and tries to protect, run away and have healthy relationships. If you believe, "I am not worthy," "I am not lovable," and you say, "I had three unsuccessful marriages, here is the proof," if your parents are arguing and you say, "Mom and Dad are fighting Something must be wrong with me?." We need to look at both sides and thinking about the relationship (ability to relate). Are they really related? If you are in that scenario, your partner can never be intimate with you. You are always on guard. Before talking about relationships, we need to talk about the relationship with ourselves. İf you come into a relationship, regardless of how open, loving, authentic or giving your partner is, if you start with a lack of trust and doubt what they are about, how will they view you? Then, you are always going to be guarded or always want control, whether that is with practical things, sex, or intimacy. There is always the element of control that will dominate and you will not be open and free. Manipulation will follow that.

You cannot give everything, you do not want to hurt, and you have to re-spot the pain inside of you. It's holding you back; trust is here. What is you actually mean with trust?? You are projecting negative intentions, setting emotions that turn to motion. This is basically the law of attraction. In this concept, the inner child want trusts and certainty.

Growing up in a dysfunctional family, or experiencing a dysfunctional childhood, can have a lasting emotional impact on our adult life. When a young child does not understand what is going on around him/her, or cannot deal with or escape from a situation which is maybe harming them emotionally, physically or mentally, the child puts this in place. If no one is guiding them or giving them emotional education on how to deal with these situations, actually the carer, educator or parents should be given emotional guidance, education is actually the one mostly causing the problem. Here is the big dilemma for child, the child is not yet capable of doing what we are doing now as an adult, talking it through and understanding it. The person that should be guiding them should be holding their hand, helping them through, and calming them for many reason. Instead, the child is left there with his/her own devices, he/she is sensitive and is creating emotional experiences and feelings because this the only way how the child knows how get attention: to seek validation or to seek approval, to get things to change. The child only knows feelings and they only creates emotional feelings.

Some kids can develop strategy to hide themselves away to avoid attention, to avoid being abused, and to avoid getting told off. They make themselves small. This is kind of an emotional pendulum. It is such an important point to note this how makes everything so complicated for so many people. There is not just one extreme to it, the child can seek attention to change or he/she can swing to the other side, battle everything inside his/her head and hide away in the corner. They can swing easily from one to another and this makes emotional education such a challenge to understand because one minute you can show one extreme and, then in a blink of an eye, right to another extreme. You have to understand the pendulum to understand the energy going on for that child, or for you. This almost like a survival strategy. We bring those strategies with us to our adulthood in the same way we those strategies with coping mechanisms in our childhood with our parents, carers, or whoever was in our environment having on influence on us. Now those strategies are affecting how we are think about ourselves as an adult and how we interact in our relationships. It affects our whole adult world.

This is mostly everything for a sensitive person, if you are reading this, you are most likely a sensitive person. It will go through that emotional filter, the emotional filter was set up when you were seven to eight years of age. You are highly intelligent, highly adaptable and can deal with anything that comes your way. You have dealt with everything that came your way, and here is the deal, emotionally you have an eight year old driving a car emotionally swerving from one side to other. Here is an example with the three lies. You know we say those three lies: "I am not good enough, I cannot cope, I am unlovable or I am not worthy," did you ever said yourself while you talk to yourself? I am sure you have, so let me put those three lies in pendulum. When you say "I am not good enough," the other extreme to that pendulum is, "I want to be slightly better, I want to be slightly superior." Do you think this sounds does not crazy? The fact is that this is real, but I will tell you the child's view on this, "If I was slightly superior, not to rub anyone's nose in it or not make anyone bad, but if they see me as slightly superior, they would better dealing with me, they would be more respectful, they would not give me such a bad time or hard time because they would treat me much better." That's the first one, I am not good enough," to, "I am slightly superior."

Using that strategy as the inner child, "I want to be perfect," "I want to be slightly better," the child does this for safety and protection. The inner child thinks, "If I prove myself to my parents or whoever is important to me, then it means I am not going to get told off. or it means they will give me love." It is not wanting to be superior for the sake of it but does have a deeper agenda actually behind it. I am sure you are saying, "Are you joking? I am the last person who wants to be superior," but think about it, and think of the benefits the pendulum gives you. If you are slightly superior, people treat you differently. They will be more respectful, they will give you a bit more space, they will honor you, they will listen to you more, so this is the emotional response to the other end of the pendulum.

The second one of other extremes is, "I cannot cope." When you say this, I want extreme here is the other extreme is, "I want to be perfect, I should be perfect, because if I'm perfect and no one be able to criticize me. They will not be able to compare me because I will be slightly superior." You see how the pendulum works now. They will not be able to be judgmental because how can anybody can be judgmental toward someone who is "perfect"? In your belief system, if you ever thought, "I should be perfect, I want to be perfect," then it is the eight year old emotionally in control.

Let's look at a picture of examples; I think it's interesting that all strategies we develop as an inner child, you can imagine a young child thinking, "I do not want to be criticized or judged." What is driven to the child, as I mentioned at the beginning, is that it wants to avoid the uncomfortable, painful red light feelings and he/she has made the association that, "When my mother criticizes me or when my father looks at me the wrong way, or when my grandparents ignore me when I do something, that makes me feel horrible. Therefore, I am going to do everything within my power as young child to avoid those feelings by seeking validation and hiding myself away so I do not get noticed." The inner child or your paradigm is working in very effective way as you see. Let's continue, when you look around yourself and even ask yourself, "Do you think are you creating those feelings?", most people will not accept they create those emotions as a response to the events. Of course, they didn't create events, they didn't create parent dysfunctionality, or they weren't dysfunctional children, but they are creating emotions. They were trying to protect themselves from emotions. They built this wall, this swinging wall like a pendulum of confusion. It is here made of confusion, a carousel of despair, self-fulfilling prophecy, they created all of there that trying protect themselves. What they actually did was keeps emotions locked in. The only thing keeping out your spirituality. You cannot connect your spirituality because you are locked in, you are in your own prison you have made. You are holding the key and this is why we use this pendulum to understand this volatile and unpredictable childhood the child created.

The third one, "I am unlovable, I am unworthy," if you ever said this to yourself, this is applies to you. That's one side of the pendulum, the opposite side is, "I want to be put on a pedestal. I really want everybody to adore me, everybody should see my true character. I am a really good girl or boy and they should see that. They should honor, respect that, and treat me accordingly. When people do not swing to the opposite side, when you do not get one side of the pendulum; you come up with this strategy. You want immediate results. This is a survival strategy for the inner child. .and we carry these survival strategies to adulthood and we let those inner child strategies rule us and our relationships. This is how we parent our own children as well.,

The other influence of a dysfunctional childhood is when we end up copying parents or environments behaviors. For example, if we reflect back on our childhood, of course, children may not be aware of this as they did not have cognitive reasoning, but we can now as an adult can reflect and say, "Oh my goodness! My father was very emotionally unbalanced and unavailable. All sorts of things were going on like drinking, substance abuse, violence, withdrawal, silent treatment, the whole spectrum of levels of destruction and abuse. In terms of our childhood experiences, we can be acutely aware of now how our parents were, what their behaviors were and how they impacted us in this way. When I spoke to people in entire my life, they say, "I am still repeating the same behaviors. I can hear myself saying my mother was saying. I did not have a good relationship with my mom and I do not have good relationships with any women due to my mom. I am doing things my father did, saying things my mother said, and I know how wrong it is." We can write plenty of these examples. Why do we this to ourselves? Through my inner child journey, I know we are making the most of ourselves in this situation. I mean the majority of us treat ourselves much worse than we were ever treated as a child. We will be unmerciful with the way we criticize ourselves, the way we dump ourselves, the way we restrict ourselves, the way we follow a familiar path, even though we know that path is not going to work. We stick to it rigidly and that's the reason why: it sounds easy, isn't it? It sounds too easy, but it can't be easy, it's more than that. Not easy , It is familiarity! And that situation or behavior familiar to the inner child, paradigm or subconscious mind, that what is trying to find a path through this. It knows that not is successful. It knows the path, it knows the outcome, it knows what going to happen, it already has the excuses, and it already has the justification. And you say "Oh you do not understand how difficult it is for me! Oh you do not realize what the world looks like! Oh Reyhan, you do not realize what the world is like!" No, I live in the world. I know what is going on and you again say "Oh, no, no, it is so much more worse for me." Here, in this moment, let's do this powerful exercise. It challenges those beliefs and those justifications. That place where you go to hide and has the excuses ripe with, "I am not good enough, I am not lovable, I cannot cope," and creates confusion for the inner child.

What do we do now?

Why do you believe you are unlovable?

Why do you believe you cannot cope?

Why do you believe you are not good enough?

Do this exercise again and again three times till you reach the roots .What is your intention is? You are trying to get to the fountainhead, the first instance. What did not come through birth cannot be delivered to this world. If you believe you are not good enough, this is something you learned. It is not natural. It is not part of you.. It is not in your cells .This is in your belief system. This exercise is the most efficient, powerful and quickest method to see where it comes from. Do not be misled by the results of thinking, Oh well, result of you say "I am unlovable because my mom left us when I was little," yes that is the result, but not the fountainhead. It is not the true source. You have to go the other way. Where did this come from? This is almost always from childhood and dysfunctional family environments, experiences and situations.

And I want to point out a couple of important aspects again because it is really powerful to have clarity and understanding on it; first, the idea of copying our parents' behavior or patterns of beliefs, actions, lifestyle, habits, even though they are wrong, we do that because of familiarity. I think the inner child is still seeking comfort, safety and protection in the familiarity. Those strategies I mentioned before protects the inner child keeping him/her safe. Copying behavior, mirroring behavior is still the inner child seeking protection, safety and comfort.

Having ignorance, not understanding he/she creates the emotions, the inner child believes the emotions are external. The inner child believes, for example, if he/she mirrors the parent and did what the parent wants, then he/she would be less likely to be annoyed, criticized or judged. This is called mnemonics. Around 70% of what children learn, not you teach them, they mimic. We mimic our environment, we copy the environment and you can do this for yourself. Think about the things you are doing, but also where you learned this behavior from. Remember the pendulum. This is where it gets confusing because you can copy your parents to the later or you can do the opposite. They say black you will say white, not because you believe white, but because they have said black. And there is the pendulum. What I am trying to do here? What do you believe and why do you believe it? Not because they believe that, I am going to believe the opposite. This still shocks them, but it does not affect them. It only affect you. It is like drinking poison and expecting them to be affected. You are the only one affected, your belief system is guiding your life, you should not believe in them. All those examples, either mirroring our parents or copying their behavior or swinging to the other extreme and going against everything they stood for just for the sake of it to prove a point, both of these extremes are actually authentic ways for us. We never stop now as an adult to think what to actually believe and what do we authentically believe. We don't think, "How I can copy parents as hard as possible so I get approval? How I can rebel against my parents or my upbringing so I can prove a point?" We never find out midway. This phrase is actually so important for your inner child's mind: to prove a point. What does this mean? A lot of people set their life by saying what was not fair, not just and what happened to them should not have to happened to them, but they are proving my point-of-view. You are awesome because you managed to come through that dysfunctionality, not understanding it and not coming to terms with it, until now, but you still came through it. How awesome is that!

This is a learned habit, this is learned behavior, this is choosing a path of familiarity, this is choosing to rebel, this is choosing to copy, and this is choosing to do survival strategies. When we no longer know what adults need to do, then this is an issue that cannot be dealt with. However, if we hold onto red light feelings of resentment, anger, unfairness or injustice about a dysfunctional childhood, that will be the block that stops us from changing. When you hold onto those beliefs, they create red light feelings, and then those red light feelings are blocking you. This is the prison you built to protect you, but it never protects you from negative emotions, whatever you want to call them (anxiety, depression, panic attacks, anger, frustration, resentment and loneliness), whatever you want to call them , why they have got so many name. But you never been protected from them. Tell me, how can you be protected from something you are continuously creating? And so what you are doing is by you are holding onto that belief, you are telling :

"They have got be paid. I am entitled. I am owed. This is should not happen to me. You do not understand my feelings, how awful it is, how hard it was...You were not here. You do not understand these feelings." You are right, I do not, but I do understand you have to go through this. Do you know how awesome you are? But now, you keep on reliving that event, and you are creating that scenario for yourself. That was 40 years ago, and now, the way you are doing it, you are bringing it into the present, and then you are creating that emotional feeling, and you are bringing into your mind. This person says, "I will not let it go. He needs to pay for it." Do you know what is the trouble with somebody paying for something? When you try to get someone to pay, you have to keep on to collecting the installments. When you try to get someone to pay for something, you are still being connected to that incident or person because you are trying to draw installments they can never pay for. They can never make it right for you, they cannot get back those moments because it is impossible. Here is a life lesson in acceptance, not accepting what they did was correct, but accepting that it happened. It is accepting how powerful, how spiritual and how awesome you are. You got through that, whether that's something extreme like abuse, bullying, split in a relationship, whether that overbearing or unbalanced parents, or whether that poor parenting techniques you suffered, you got through it. That's how awesome you are! Do not drag it along with you like an anchor that's weighing you down. Let it go, let it go! Accept how awesome you are to be able to have gotten through that. This shows me fortitude is one of your greatest assets, to be determined to get on with your life, to hold on the past and this spiritual lesson, the life lesson, you have got to change. You are reaching a sense of peace with the situation somehow. If you can accept and move on, but the inner child always resists what we need to do here, you need to find out why the inner child resist firstly, you need to get answers for this because inner child will want to go down the old familiar path. The game that you play with the inner child is to make new way familiar, and you will be surprised how quickly this happens.

I am not talking about years, I am talking about weeks or months. Here is another important point or lesson: consistency. Once you do not rush to make a decision, and be self-responsible, once you absolutely accept 100% you create every emotional experience and feeling, then you are consistent with your child. When you start to have, what I call, squealing piglets and it is like your child walking down for chocolate in the supermarket, you have to be consistent and not be drawn into their game. This is the way out. Do not let the inner child take you to the extremes. Hold center ground with what you know is right, what do you believe and why you believe it. That's so important in taking responsibility. It is your life and this is your journey. I want you in control of it, you can do it. I am only here to show you the truth. The only person who can change is you! Beliefs are not set in stone. You can transform those faulty beliefs with consistency and repetition. Affirmation to your subconscious mind means sitting and having a talk with your inner child.

CHAPTER FIVE

FEAR OF INTIMACY: RELATIONSHIPS

"Even death is not to be feared by one who has lived wisely." "The whole secret of existence is to have no fear. Never fear what will become of you, depend on no one. Only the moment you reject all help are you freed."

- Buddha

We want love, why wouldn't we? I think the best thing ever is to have someone to come home to, someone that's got your back. Along with love, we want intimacy. Intimacy is amazing, but most of us are fearful of intimacy. Now, I want to tell you how to overcome the fear of intimacy. You may ask why would anyone have a fear of intimacy because when you are intimate with someone; you are so bonded, you are so connected. Here is the problem. When we talk about our most of intimate moments , it can be sexual, but it does not only mean that The first person you had an intimate relationship with was a parent, because intimacy does not mean having sex, understand this first. When we talk about our most of intimate moments, it can be sexual, but it does not only mean that. If people who loved you, or were supposed to love you, hurt and abused you emotionally, physically, sexually, withheld from you, or were mean to you; now, you have a very confusing message about what love and intimacy is. If the person you are supposed to bond with and connect to, has disappointed and hurt you, you did not stop loving them, but you stop loving yourself.

An intimate relationship for you in this stage means, "I am going to love you, you are going to love me, but I do not love myself, and if I do not love myself, how on earth can I believe that you love me? If I think I am not good enough and you think I am amazing, either I do not believe you or I cannot accept it." We learn what we live and then we set about recreating what we learned. The inner child has something that I find immensely vexing, the inner child needs to run back to what it is super familiar with, while running away from what is unfamiliar. You start to say:

"I had cold, distant, diminishing parents and all my partners have been cold, distant and diminishing. My dad cheated on my mom and he never give her any money, and that's so weird I seem to like guys that cheat and never get their wallet out."

Why is that? Well, there are a couple of things as to why this is so, you learn what you live; your inner child programmed all things, and then you try to recreate those emotional experiences again. Then, another way to go about this, you try to change the ending of what you learned and lived. And you start to say:

"I am going to find a cold person and turn them into a warm lovely pussycat. I am going to find a mean person and make them super generous, I am going to find someone who is emotionally unstable to express their feelings and have them write me poetry."

Life is way too short to change the endings. You need to change beginnings, so let's imagine you have a fear of intimacy and you want to get over it. I am going to ask you some questions and I want you answer while you are reading these phrases or at least make a note of what they are.

What did you learn about love growing up?

Where did you learn your beliefs about love?

You see, a lot of people will have same the experience with a different belief.

There is great example here many of you would be agree on he said, "My mother loved me so much, and it was oppressive, it was suffocating. I was her everything, she depended on me, I was her little prince and while it was lovely to be loved, it was also horrible. She did not give my dad a look. It was all me, me, me, me, me! And then she has a lot of guilt, "I will die if you are not here, you are the only one who makes me happy." Now, I found a girlfriend and she starts to say the same thing, "I only want to be with you," like that song, "I only want to be with you, you are my everything." Although I love her and she is amazing, a part of mind goes, "Oh my god, this is my mom all over again." She suffocates me and she smothers me with love. "Now, I have got this great girl and she is doing the same thing. Where is the door? I just want to get out"

Other people would say "what I learned about love is my parents were miserable, they fought all the time, but they stayed together and I asked them, "Why?" they said, "Well, we made our vows. What would the next door neighbors think?" and what I learned about love was; you stick it out no matter what. You pay a terrible price for that kind of love. Other people say, "No, my parents did not stick it out. My dad left and he had so many relationships; my mom too. They were both serial cheaters and one of them was. Now, I found someone and my fear is, 'Oh my god, what if it does not last and I am stuck?' or, 'What if it does last and I am like other people I have to stay in this relationship forever?' "

These are good questions to ask yourself, don't you think? What did I learn about love? Where did I learn about love? How bonded was I to my mother? How bonded was I to my father? What did they show me in actions and words that were destructive, damaging or limiting? Why do I believe their relationship is the template I am forced to follow by the inner child? So ask yourself those questions, and then realize because you learned that, it does not have to be your life.

Let's look at this example, I know some of you say, "My father and my mother were so unsuited. My mother was so beautiful, stunning and gorgeous, and I think my father was completely smitten on a superficial level. She was very sexy, very dramatic, very flamboyant, but he was very cerebral and academic. I have no idea what they had in common, but their marriage was not a happy marriage. I remember watching their relationship and thinking, 'You know what? When I grow up, I need to have a really engrossing job because my father was a head teacher, if I have that, it's okay when my relationship goes wrong." Notice that I said, "when" not "if". I said, "When, not I suppose, that all relationships are a disaster because I saw that every day growing up, and I decided a good engrossing career is the cure. My sister saw the same thing and she said 'You must find someone who loves you more than you love them and they will never leave you.' My brother saw the same thing and he thought, 'Never go for hysterical, beautiful women like that because they are difficult and impossible.' Each of us saw exactly the same relationship being played out with the calm, logical, career-driven father and the beautiful, but hysterical mother. We saw the same thing, but we formed different beliefs: "Always put your career first", "Do not marry beautiful women", "Do not marry someone unless they love you way more than you love them because they will never leave you", "We each took something."

Take a minute now and think about what you took from your

parents relationship. What did you take from them that colored, shaped and formed your beliefs about relationships? Were you brought up by cheaters, people who stuck it out, people who complained all the time, people who were always talking about what they missed out on? Or did you have parents who were so amazing, in love, and connected that you thought, "I can never find that," and everything was going to be disappointing because you compared everything to them? That's the first thing to do. Have a look at what you learned? Remember, you learned what you live, and then you recreate it, while you are trying to change the endings. One of my friends told me a story, he went to show his mother a painting and she said, "Darling, you might be six, please remember, I am not six. I find you terribly boring. I should never have been a parent. I am far too intelligent to relate to you and I find children boring. I really should not have had any." This is an awful thing to say to your kids, I think. Guess what kind of women he liked? Super intelligent intellectuals who have always made him feel bad about himself. He was trying to get the love his mother did not give him by finding women just like his mother. And trying to make them love him. I said, "Look, here is your clue. Whenever you meet a women ask yourself one question, "How do I feel about myself with this women or man?" If the answer is, "A bit stupid or they are so intelligent," think about this relationship it is really for you or not?!" He later said, "You know, I heard you in my head saying that and one day I met this girl and I suddenly thought, "Wow, I feel so intelligent with her." He married her and they are still very happy together.

Some of us say, "You know, my father said I was just like my mother. I would amount to nothing and I am attracted to men who say that too. And then I try to make them love me." Love should not be earned, run after, bought, or worked for. It should be just there! Remember this pattern: learn what you live, (the inner child always tends to go a familiar route), try to replicate it and try to change the endings. Don't try to make a cold diminishing person warm, make a withholder generous, make a cheater faithful, make a bad boy loyal, make an unattainable woman only want you. Stop trying to change the endings, life is too short. Change the beginnings. If you can do that, you will overcome all your fears of intimacy. But what does intimacy even mean? It means "into-me-you-see", in-ti-ma-cy. Many of us say, "You know what? I have gone through life but I have put on an act. I pretend I am confident. I pretend I am all that. I pretend I am happy. I fake it. I go out with people and say "Hey I am great, I have a great job, I have a great life, I have it all together" and I can fake it, but it's really hard to fake it all the time." We can all go out in the evening and put on an act, but when you are with someone all the time, they see the real you. Intimacy means, "I see the real you with your flaws." I see you when you have a cold, flu, headache or when your hair is mess, or you had a challenging day. Then we have this fear, "Oh I can fake it and expect you to like that fakeness, but when I show you the real me, what if you do not like the real me?" because we are all told a lie. We like people who are perfect glossy, shiny and amazing, and if you can present the perfect image to someone, they will love you. You know that's not true. You know at the base of relationships, we choose people who share our vulnerability. We like people who have the same vulnerabilities as us, and then when we bond and connect. Do you know what perfect people do not have? They do not have bonding. They are very often alone, they are usually very unhappy because they are pretending to be something that does not exist. You cannot be perfect. You know you can be the best you can be and the best you can be is a really flawed person having a flawed relationships with another flawed person. I am flawed, my friend is flawed, our kids are flawed, our partner are flawed, our relatives are flawed, and it makes it so much easier to love them and accept them because we all have flaws. Some people say, "I love my partners flaws, I love the fact that when they undress, they have a little fat tummy because now I can have little fat tummy," or "I love the fact that they are forgetful or they have got a bit of temper because it allows me to not be perfect." It would be an awful thing to have a partner who is perfect because do how that would make you feel? Inadequate, always inadequate so forget about it. Finally, we do this thing too, which is, "I am going to find someone and they are going to make me feel amazing, I am going to find this perfect person. They are going to make me feel so good about myself." If you give someone out there the power to make you feel good and complete you, you give them the power to take that away anytime they like, deliberately or unintentionally. Love can make us feel very vulnerable. "I love this person so much, they are my world, and I am nothing without them. If they die, well, I don't know if I could go on. If this person left me, that's would be the end of world." There is no doubt relationships do complete you, but if you give you someone power to make you worthwhile, you give them power to take that away. You have to love yourself, believe yourself and love your relationship. If that ended, you would be terribly sad, maybe bereft, but you would continue because the person that completes you is YOU. The final problem with the intimacy is "Oh I was doing great, but now I am so vulnerable, now I am dependent, now I have all these feelings; I am jealous, I am irrational, I am moody. I was never jealous before, I was not irrational, I was not vulnerable." When you really love someone, it does make you vulnerable because you love them so much. How do you overcome it? First of all, you stop what you are trying to recreate, the same emotional experiences (what you lived), stop trying to change the endings and change the beginnings. Stop running back to what is familiar. The inner child loves, wants and tends to familiarity. Run away from that; run towards what is unfamiliar. Make what is unfamiliar, familiar to you, and then decide, "You know what? It does make me vulnerable to love, but I would rather be vulnerable than not." Do you know the expression, "It is better to have loved and lost, than never to have loved before"? Finally, if you have a deep love, deep intimacy, you create a template and should anything happen to that relationship, should that partner die or leave you, because you have a template for love, you will find love again. It is people who never have loved who find it harder. When you do have love or if you have loved and lost, please remember something amazing the person who called you and said, "Oh my God, you are so great. I just ring your number to hear your voice. I love everything about you. You are the one; you are amazing." When the relationship goes wrong, they do not pack those things up and, ,they do not take them away. They are still in you; everything your ex loved about you and adored about you is still there. They do not have the power to remove it, when they go it is still in you. If they saw that in you, the next person will see it too. Every relationship that does not work out teaches you what does work and what does not work.

Every relationship that does not work makes the next one far more likely to work because you learned something. Sharing our vulnerabilities is bonding that's why people in Alcoholics Anonymous (AA) bond to a group because no one in AA says, "I am so great. I am so cool." They say, "No, you know, I sold my kids dollhouse to buy a drink. I did some terrible things to buy a drink. I stole from my employer." and we respond, "I like you. You are real, , you re authentic and you know what you say. I did the same as well, and now, I can bond with you and you can bond with me because we are both being real." It is a great thing when you can be yourself and let the person who loves you love be real and authentic with you. Let them see your flaws just as you see their flaws, and how much your parents hurt you, wounded you, and withheld from you. You have to get over that because if you do not fix your inner child wounds, you bleed all over people who never cut you. Take some time to heal your paradigm or inner child by saying, "My mom was not the greatest, my dad was absent, but you know what? Nobody wakes up and thinks, "Right, how can l ruin my kid's life?" They did the best they could, it was pretty rubbish really, but they were victims of their own childhoods too. They learned that. They did not have the ability to transform and heal their inner child, and I do not have to carry this around with me anymore. I am not going to drag a big case around the world with my childhood wounds and beliefs. I am not going to bleed on people who did not inflict those cuts on me in the first place. I am going to get over it." Human beings are remarkably resilient and, to be happy, you have to forgive the past. Reconciliation needs to happen between you and your inner child. You need to feel great about the present, grateful for the present and really excited about the future. Love is all around you; it is available. Being intimate is wonderful, you can have deep intimate love a fantastic erotic sex life, great friendships; and it has nothing to do with how you started in life. It does not matter where you come from. It is where you are going that counts. You are driving the car now, and you can go where ever you want. You can certainly love, stay in love, be intimate , and keep that going for your entire life. Complete yourself, I highly recommend it. Fall in love with yourself, become intimate with who you are and it will be easier to do that with everyone else too. Love yourself because you are awesome and good enough!

CHAPTER SIX

HOW TO LET GO OF PAST HURT

"Be grateful for whoever comes and goes, because each has been sent as a guide from beyond."

- Rumi

Are you holding onto past issues that are affecting your health and happiness? Maybe you are stuck with feelings of injustice or unfairness, and you are not just willing to forgive or forget, or maybe you are hurt like a child stubbornly holding on and not wanting to let go of past issues. Why does our inner child keep us in the past and what does he/she believe is the payoff for doing this? The healing power of acceptance rather than forgiveness and, most importantly, how you can work with your inner child so that you can finally release old hurt?

I will start with a example case and question. Probably, this case or question will be so familiar to you and every one of us:

"I cannot stop ruminating in the past, how badly I was treated as young child and my many failed relationships as an adult. I look around me and see all my contemporaries who came from loving homes are successful and happy. I do not deserve more, especially after my disadvantaged early years. The injustice and unfairness of it all is gnawing away at me. I know this is unhealthy, but I am stuck in my past and there is nothing I can do to change it, can you help?"

Well, this is a great question, a very powerful question. It just shows you the childhood experiences and what a profound effect that has on your belief system or your thinking, therefore, your life. When we go through these childhood experiences, we see how this really affect us on a very deep level. I think it is much deeper than we give it credit for. I do not think we realize just how impactful it is, especially on an emotional level. This is what I want to get into in this question because what you are talking about there is what we class as inner child work. Just as a reminder, inner child trauma or work is between the ages zero to eight years and it seems to be very relevant here. When you are growing up around these ages, when things were happening in your life that created very powerful emotional feelings, in other words, you knew it was not right, but could not understand what was going on. It did not give you a good feeling, spiritually, it upset you. What sort of typical situations I am talking about here? It can be very serious situations like abuse ;physical, emotional or sexual based. It could be what other people would think were not so serious like split ups in our families, moving from home, changing schools or losing friends. It can be a number of things, but for a child, particularly for a sensitive child, something has happened. It could also be one thing or it can be a series of events that upset the child within you. The child is experiencing emotions they do not understand yet that they are creating. They believe the emotions are coming externally into them like when you see in films where a storm of arrows come flying in. It is like a rain of emotions flying in at them. The child does the only thing that is really left open for the child to do: protect themselves the way they know at that age. The child puts up a barrier, builds a wall and, when the emotions keep coming in, he/she builds the wall higher and higher and higher. This question is revolving around that issue. If you were with me now, I would ask you more questions. I would be almost sure that if you looked at that period around those ages, you would see things were happening in your life that you did not understand or could not comprehend, and you turned into yourself and then built the wall for a lockdown.

As an educator, having experience with different age groups of children really gave me this idea that all children I meet till now, and I can say almost all children, want to please their parents. They want to be validated, adored, reassured and old that their parents are proud of them. If for any reason, for instance the parent cannot do that because of their own emotional issues, they cannot support them in the way that the child believes he/she should be or asked. You look at your friends at school and you see them going home and their mommies baked them nice cookies, waited for them and sat down to talk to them, and then you go home to problems, arguments and perhaps emotional issues. You as a child, how many times have you heard yourself say, "It is not fair! It is not fair! They are getting something that I am not getting." I want you to think about that phrase. How many times have you heard maybe your physical child say that? How many times have you said that in that part of your mind, the inner child?

I want to rebrand and change rather that "it is not fair" to, "it is not the way I believe it should be". "I looked at my friends and I see them having a better family life. I see their parents supporting them. I see their dads coming to parent evening and my dad does not even talk to me, he refuses to acknowledge me, and that's not fair." What you saying is it is not the way I want it to be and for a child this is immense. I am not underestimating this because a child now is encountering almost a premature life lesson. He/she is encountering the situation, but it is really above their pay grades because they do not have the cognitive reasoning to understand his/her mother and father has their own emotional issues. Why would a child think that? Most children think that whatever their parents say is true. Ask yourself if what is always your parents always say is true. Now, probably you know as an adult, that was not true. You can probably see, if you are a parent yourself, that it was not true. However, as a child, you believe everything that comes out of your parents' mouths is probably the truth and should be listened to, so try to please your parents or placate your parents. When they were unhappy, your parents are maybe even blamed you. If they said, "If I did not have all these kids around me, I would be happy," then you start to blame yourself, "It must be me, there must be something wrong with me. I am not living up to their standards." This is what creates all the problems if you think, "What they are saying is my fault because if I was this perfect child, then everything else would be all right so the world would be just and fair. I would get what I want and my parents would be happy with me all the time because I would deliver what they wanted."

If you say "I was a perfect child, I was not a bad child, I would do what my parents wanted," but the problem is you cannot do what they want. You cannot be that perfect child because a perfect child does not exist. That's why what they said is a conditioned the way of thinking and it is incorrect, but we cannot blame the child because the child is very young. They cannot blame the child because they don't have that reasoning developed yet. The child ends up creating something very powerful, I call it the vow, to himself/herself, "It must be me. The fault lies with me. I am faulty. There is something wrong with me." When you have that belief that I find with a lot of people, what I call the core beliefs and dig down to ask the three key questions, it goes down to, "I am not good enough, I cannot cope, and I am not lovable." When you get down to the core, what they are saying is, "something for T in me. I am NOT awesome. I am not divine. I am missing something. I have to do something to work hard to earn love and validation. If I do not get it, it is not their fault, it is my fault because I have not worked hard enough."

The child is almost putting the cart in front of the horse. The child is thinking the wrong way and believes that he/she has to earn this validation. Constantly, the child is looking for the rest of his/her life because that filter is set up. The child is looking for this validation and reassurance, looking to be told that he/she is loved, worthy, and then, it is never enough, is it? It is almost like you can never be validated quite enough. You can never be loved quite enough and as you get older, you say, "It is very difficult to have relationship because even if your partners tell you that you are gorgeous, they love you, they want to be with you, that little voice of the inner child will awaken and wonder, "Do they really mean it? They are going to change their mind." They start playing this really toxic game of testing them. "Let me give them a test. Let me just test them. Let me just test them. Have they passed? Let me test them a little bit more," and this becomes all the stuff I mentioned in other chapters: the carousel of despair, the maze of confusion, strategies and manipulations.

I want to be absolutely clear on this for most of us, when we are young typically between these ages, something happens to us and give us strong emotional or red light feelings, either an uncomfortable series of things or events that could be abuse, strong issues, bullying, upsets in the family, your siblings being favored over you or you looking at your friends and thinking their parents are treating them better than yours. These are all sorts of things which create red light feelings that children then blame themselves in their mind :"It must be me, something wrong with me," and their the inner child gives themselves vow and then creates this pervasive sense of unfairness and injustice with calling: "If I was a good girl or if I was a good boy, then everything would be right. Everything would be nice, people would love me and people would care for me. I would be enough for my parents." and to take it one step further, the child is trying hard as hard as he/she can but cannot make it right, and says, "It is not fair I am trying harder than my friends and they get what I do not get. How is it fair? It just does not make sense myself " As you see the situation how becomes like a carousel of despair for her/him. There is no answer for them because they might try harder and think, "No matter what I do or say, the situation still exists, therefore, it is me. I just cannot do this." We all have or had those feelings, thoughts and beliefs as a child. They are so shocking to us and profoundly resonate with who we are that they then get locked into our psyche or mindset, and that then becomes the what I call the inner child. That inner child part of our mind is what we carry into adulthood.

What I want to emphasize is the inner child part of you becomes a filter, like a coffee machine, everything goes through that, including your experience as an adult. Everything. The partners you choose, the job you do, the way you live and the way you think about yourself is going through that filter that was developed as a child. That is why I believe the analogy of the inner child works really well because, in a way, that inner child is still in control. That little child is still trying to achieve right from wrong by becoming good enough to make everything fair to get back to what believes he/she was old because it did not get the fairness that as a child.

Let's go with this and say, "If my parents would have been wonderful, wouldn't it be better? Wouldn't it be great if I did come home and my milk and cookies were waiting for me. If mommy had bounced me on her knee and told me how much she loved me, then I would have been successful, wouldn't I? Because I would have had that grounding, that base, and I did not have that and, therefore, that is the reason why I am not successful." It is blame culture. It is also blaming in the sense of, "I am a victim of my childhood circumstances or my past circumstances and there is nothing I can do about it. It is almost like I'm now emotionally handicapped. Now, I am disadvantaged for the my rest of life so I am owed big time." And in return, I ask you, "Who owes you this?" You are looking for other people or the situations or the jobs. You are looking around and when you get something, it is never quite enough, is it? You always want something more. It is almost like a dog chasing. This is what I call the carousel of despair because you are chasing, chasing, chasing and wanting more, but you are never satisfied. You are always thinking there is something else, if -everything was just perfect, for instance, this is a great example now, "If I just did everything right, then everyone would understand, they would treat me differently, and I would get my justice. Then, I would get what I deserve and what I am entitled to." It is always this wanting, wanting, wanting and, because of the childhood experiences, that's why this is such a good question at the beginning of the chapter. In the question you said, "I cannot change it" because it happened, but you are right we cannot change what happened, and here is the life lesson, the spiritual teaching, we cannot change what happened but you can change your perception of what happened. We cannot change if you are right, you were raised in a dysfunctional home, with a dysfunctional family, or with dysfunctional parents, we cannot change that. We cannot wave a magic wand and make it right for you and retrace your steps to have the milk and cookies ready for you. We cannot change that, but we can change the perception because the perception is yours. I telling you that you are proving my point. You are a spiritual being, you are proving that you are awesome, you are proving that you are divine. The proof is that you got through those dysfunctional situations and relationships. You got through that, now, what did you learn from that? What is it that you can do in your mind? What is it you can do in your belief system so that situation will never occur and come to you ever again? How can you change that? There is a spiritual lesson and that's something you can do. This is the really empowering part for me because as a child you were not in control of what was going on. You were just a child, a youngster. You weren't in control, that is reality, but now you are and in control you can take responsibility. Now, you can authentically reflect on what happened and decide what you are going to do about it, and you can say what is the authentic lesson here. You can ask yourself, "What does this tell me about the emotional perception of my parents or the kind of practical upbringing I had?" Here is the teaching of this part: the past does not define you unless you allow it to because the past is just that. It is the past.

I do not know how long ago, I do not know how old you are, but let's say it was 20-30 years ago. Why are you bringing the past into the present? Why are you making something that happened 20 or 30 years ago an issue? Is it even relevant to what happening in your life now? Who is the only person that's doing that? You are in your perception, in your belief system. This is why all of these spiritual teachings are all about taking self-responsibility, understanding your beliefs, what you believe and why you believe it. See, you are actually almost reliving the past in the carousel of despair. You are reliving those experiences every day, in every relationship and in every way you think about yourself. Why do not let it go? Because it is only you doing it and here is what I noticed when I work with dysfunctional families, and sometimes I do bring them together, the parents are horrified. It did not even register with them what they were doing was wrong because they were in an emotional situation. Normally, you hear the story about what you did not realize. They were going through problems like being on the edge of divorce or whatever else. The parents are horrified because they heard from their children, the only ones that have this movie replaying in their minds. You are going over it and everything, you are so good with this movie. You have kind of owned the movie. The movie is not you and it is in the past 20 , 30, 40, 50 years ago . It has no relevance. Unless, you give it relevance in your life right now. This is such a profound and important spiritual teaching: take control of your life; live your life now. If you went through that dysfunctional type of childhood, well done, congratulations! You should stick your chest out and you should say, "Look up! I got through that." I know nobody will ever understand how difficult it was for you. We all have a story. I have a story, which is this book. Parts of my story are in it with fruits of my healing and journey that I am sharing with you. I was there one upon time and I have been through all of that, believe me. I had experiences just like you. I got through it, you got through it, and we are here now. That is the proof of the way. This is the proof of how awesome and divine that you are. Even a dysfunctional childhood, even the people that you depend on to nurture you, to nourish you, they could not do that. You got through it. You did that! Why would you keep on going back over the whole thing? And you came up with this answer:

"I can kind of tell why I do it because almost like as an adult you know that being angry, bitter, resentful, anxious (all these red light feelings) and all these thoughts associated with what happened in the past, you know it is not good for you. You know, most people kind of know that is not helping them to live their greatest potential. Logically, you know that, but then there is that part of you, the inner child, that stubbornly holds on to it. I really want to let go. I know it is not helping me at all. I want to move on, but it is like a heavy rock, and if I let it go, I am letting go of all the past stuff like it never happened. But I want people to know that I had a bad childhood. I want people to know how bad it was."

Tell me why you think like that?

"Because I want people to understand that if I make a mistake or if I fail, it is because I was disadvantaged. I had a poor start. It is almost like my get-out-of-jail card, but it is not imaginary. It is like this is all disadvantageous. I had it, but if I let it go, then I am on the back foot again with my life, I will not feel protected again. I have no justification."

You explained it well. Do you recognize this? I call this medals of honor. I have witnessed this with many people. I will give you quick story. Many years ago, I met a man in a public place and I was waiting my turn to buy something to eat. He was just behind me, a 70-80 year old man, standing a broth with a blazer and white flannels. He had all his war medals on him to come to buy some food. Well, of course, when we were waiting we greeted each other and started speaking. I had to ask him about his medals and he spent all of the waiting time explaining what each of these medals were. It was very interesting and I enjoyed talking to him. He got really involved telling me, "Well, this year I got this on the battlefield here... and I got this for this, and I got this... " Finally, I had to stop him to get my food. If I did not stop now, I would not get my food and do my other stuff. After me, he bought his food and I never saw him again. Afterwards, I sat and I thought, "Why did he have to wear his medals on his back in daily life and outside?" He had to tell me, "You are speaking to someone a little bit different here. You are speaking somebody with a big history. I am somehow a little bit special. I am just a little bit different than the normal 70-80 year old man. This is my story. I want you know my story." This is why I believe you cannot get on with life like this man. It is like your story is defining you.

You want this story and when you look at the story, you want people to realize a couple of things about you so they cut you a bit of slack. There is a little excuse if things do not go well. You can tell this to yourself, even if you do not blame yourself , because a lot of people think, "I never tell anybody," but you are telling yourself. Remember, self-talk is a conversation with the universe. You are telling yourself, "Well, I did not quite do that because of my childhood," and I believe this is one big reason why you do not want to let go of past hurt because if you let go, then you have to take responsibility. I often say this, and if this is you or you can recognize anything that we talk about, just quietly ask yourself after this part; close your eyes, drop your shoulders, take a deep breath and just say, "If I didn't have my childhood, if I my life started today, ,my life started right now what would it be like?" Obviously, that is quite a big meditation, but when I do that with people I work with, I take them through a five minute meditation. Then, they always say, "Oh, it would not be so much better, I'd be lighter." Then, why don't you do it? Why don't you live now authentically and truthfully? I know, honestly why waste your life, your time, your effort , your sleep. Why keep running this movie through your mind? It will never change. You cannot change your past. Here is the spiritual teaching: your past is the past. You will read about forgiveness after this part. I do not like to call forgiveness because it puts you on a higher or lower level. It is hierarchical and I much prefer the teaching of acceptance. You just drop your shoulders and accept it, just accept this is your story! This was your journey and the evidence of how awesome you are is that you have come through that story. You have come through it, and you have lived through it. You have learned your lessons and that is acceptance. Just let it go. Forgiveness means, I think, I am not judging them as having done something wrong. I mean, it is not the point. I am not saying deny what happened or ignore what happened. I am not saying at all. I am not saying, most importantly, it was okay that it happened. No, no. That is not acceptable. It was wrong, it was dysfunctional, and it should have never happened. Whether that is abuse or a dysfunctional childhood, I am absolutely agreeing with you. I am saying it was wrong it should not have happened . It is part of your journey, accept that. , just accept ,You came through it and now you can make a choice whether you want to leave it all or if you want to keep on carrying it with you. That is the question, do you want to have it like a rucksack on your back, feeling like you are carrying around heavy rocks?

You say, "If I knew when you say that, I just like let go in those moments of dirt so I have a sense of lightness, but I know what happens a few days later, a few hours later or a few weeks later; those feelings, the red light feelings associated with injustice, unfairness, bitterness, anger, disappointment and feeling not good enough, come back."

You do the why, why, why because as you get down to the inner child, you would say, "It is not fair; it is not just," and what do we say to the inner child?

Because the inner child part of you is still holding on. Be aware that this part of you is really stubborn! The meditation for that day or those couple of days or times you say, "Okay my darling, I would say as okay my darling, okay sweetie okay, so on .I hear you, let's go through it... " and you sit with your child and meditate. I think meditation is a way of focusing your mind and you give yourself 10-20 minutes to go through what the child still wants to talk about, "It's not fair, my mommy should not have done that, my dad should not have done that and my school should not have done that. It was wrong to be bullied," and this is the life lesson or the spiritual teaching; that is the life lesson you have to learn to answer the child, and you have to give the child a reasonable answer. The child will go away, chew it over for a couple of weeks, they do not accept it quite rightly, and come back to you. The child will do the squealing piglet or have a temper tantrum ;it is not fair , it is not fair. All that means is they have not accepted it all. Like with any child, you go back and you give the child the information to digest so he/she can speak to you. It shows that you can argue with you. And what you are doing I call this reparenting or showing compassion to the inner child. There is a part specially for this topic in this book as well. As the adult to the part you see as a child, you should be acting in the way that the child wanted his/her physical parents to act. Here is the key now, for a lot us, guess what we are doing? We are acting exactly the same dysfunctional way as our parents did to us. This is what breaks the circle. The child part of your mind will test you. My goodness, I mean it will take you to the edge because it knows in the past how to push you right to the edge, guess what? You can't give in. It will push you, when you are doing this inner child work, but you should never give in. Find the answer, go to your community, get the help, do the meditation, do the affirmation and whatever resonates with you, then go back and give the child the explanation. Give the child the answer to the question in the way a physical parents should have because you are giving the child what it wants; attention, reassurance and validation. You are answering his/her questions and you are saying the most important thing, "I am going to listen to you and I am going to answer your questions. If I do not know the answer, I am going to be honest with you; I am going to go find the answer, and I am going to come back, even if you do not like the answer, I am still going to give it to you. We have to do this together as a team," and this is the reparenting. It is really important not act in the way that your parents acted with you. Act a spiritually sensitive person by being patient, calm, and peaceful. Then, your child will test you because the child will go, "All right, let's see how good you are at this," and then he/she will test you, and once you give in and you say, "There you are. Look, I do not know about your crap. You are rubbish, you are not good enough, you are stupid, and you are lazy," how many times have you said these things to yourself? The child locked in you told you this, and that is why this inner child work can be so powerful if it is done correctly.

I think the idea of fairness and unfairness; just and unjust; to forgive and to not forgive; to be entitled and to not be entitled; and right and wrong, these black and white things, are the pendulum. It is very much how a child thinks, but to be honest this is how we are taught about life as a child. We are taught if you are a good girl or boy and, if you behave nicely, then you will get a reward. There is the entitlement set up. If somebody says or does something bad to you, then I will make it better. There is the kind of righting the wrong, justice and injustice, or they are not behaving nicely so do not do what they do because they will get their comeuppance. We teach our children these things, and I think it is perpetuated by our society in our media this idea of justice and injustice. If we do X, Y and Z then surely we are entitled to this, so we get these kind of black and white extreme teachings as a child. Our parents tried to help us or kept trying to keep us on the straight and narrow, but it polarizes our thinking. Then, that reinforced by our thinking as adults and by our society. When we are doing the reparenting work, we have to say, "You know, sometimes challenging and extreme events will happen and the life lessons are how you deal with them." Not that they are right, but they will not always necessarily be wrong. Some people are not perfect for you, and if they are not, they do not behave well according to you; it is because they have their own problems, or they have their own misunderstandings. Their behavior is not necessarily going to change, or they are not necessarily going to come back to you and ask for forgiveness. The whole teaching of forgiveness is another big one because a lot of people advocate this idea of forgiving yourself, forgiving all the people and that creates a sense of who is the judge and jury; who is the criminal; and who determines who is the one to say, "You have done enough to make it okay." Acceptance is much more self-empowering, much more about self-responsibility and much more about what is right. What I can do about this now? How I can move on with my life positively?

We use love as a commodity as to praise or to withdraw and we are not surprised, well why we are surprised, as a child we see things in that way. I pointed out black and white, good and bad, yes and no because that's what we tell them. My point is here is a different way of doing it. Instead of trying to correct the old way, look at it through a different lens. Look at it through your spiritual self, and, if you came from a dysfunctional family or a dysfunctional situation, oh my goodness it is now your responsibility to be functional. That is your responsibility. Do not blame them; they were not functional and that does not mean you have to be dysfunctional as well. You do not have to copy them. You have to rise to your true self, and you have to be at one with you. You have to love, nourish and cherish yourself. This is not selfish. Everything your mom and dad said to you was not the truth. If you are a mom or dad, ask yourself if everything you say to your children 100% the truth. It is not because we are human beings and we are not perfect. We should be teaching our children self-responsibility to learn how to make decisions; to learn if they get something wrong, they can be corrected; to learn it is okay not to be perfect; it is okay to get things wrong; and to learn lessons. This is not bad. Do not punish yourself and them if they get things wrong. Ask them what they learned from that and, if you make that slight tweak from the mortal to spirituality, it is very practical, something you can use every day to live in your truth; to live honestly; to live with integrity; to have a clear path of what you are trying to achieve; and to understand that has twists and turns in that road; and then above all to take self-responsibility. You are not perfect and I think it would be terribly boring to be perfect. We all have flaws, so accept yourself and everyone with their flaws. This is perfectly perfect.

CHAPTER SEVEN

FORGIVENESS OR ACCEPTANCE

"Yesterday I was clever, so I wanted to change the world. Today I am wise, so I am changing myself."

- Rumi

If we have done something that is considered wrong or an extreme mistake in the past that we cannot undo, it is like there is no answer. There is no resolution. It becomes like an internal torture, then we cannot resolve this problem. This is why people struggle so much to let go of what they have done to forgive themselves. So many times we hear that we have to learn self-forgiveness, but it becomes an impossible task. How do we find our way through this? First, we have to cut that down a little bit, if we have done things we regret in the past, well, that's everyone have we not? You are not alone. There is not one person sitting out there and reading this, when they look back at their life, regardless if it is a small or big regret, they had an event or situation they regret. I do not think it is bad to get things wrong as you learn the lesson because if you do not learn the lesson, guess what happens? You just repeat them and you go around and around and around again. To the best of my ability, I will not never make mistake twice. Of course, because I am human, but I will tell you I am very focused on the misunderstandings and the things I got wrong to make sure to the best of my ability that will not happen again. But to emphasize this, we only learn by making mistakes so you cannot sit there and say, "I have never made a mistake," because that would not be right. We all make mistakes so the spiritual lesson is that you learn from the mistake. These mistakes or misjudgments, whatever you want to call it, they could be something relatively mild or something quite serious. The point is everything is on a spectrum. There is always a life lesson to learn even if what we did was done intentionally and, for the some people, perhaps they knew what they were doing at that time was not the right thing to do. Y, they still did it. That is very important because that's what I call the justification. If you are doing something, and you may be doing it now, that you know is incorrect and not right for you, whatever you are going to call it is not authentic. Whatever word you want to use it instead because I know everybody get different. I am trying to get to that misjudgment, then there will be the justification you offer yourself to enable you to do that and that's when you learned life lessons.

Then, reflect back and see that you know the reasons why you did that to yourself and potentially to others. That's where the lesson is because it was not authentic, it was not truthful, it was not infused with integrity, and it goes against the spiritual contract with yourself. Basically, what is that? "What I did in that time was not following my higher self, and it was not following my spiritual truth. It was following my human- centered mind, my ego, my inner child's demands, desires and fears," and you say, "It is not fair. , you deserve ,they deserve their own back," It does not matter what other people think, the human-centered mind will give you all of the justification and that is the really deeper lesson there. If you look back at those whatever we going to call them judgements, mistakes or wrongdoings, it is very important to acknowledge them first. It is very important to know what you did was wrong and accept that! You could have done better. Then, the real lesson, this is where you can only do this working with someone, is asking why did you justify this and what were the excuses, if you prefer that word, because that is what you have to learn. If you do not learn that, you are allowing your human centered mind and inner child to be in control of your life and then you are victim.

The problem with this is when people say, "I have this internal torture going on. I cannot forgive myself. I cannot forget the past." You are allowing the human centered mind to berate you and the ego to constantly torture you with regret, guilt, shame, etc. You are not spending all that time and energy thinking about what a bad person you are, but you are not actually learning the life lesson. You are just on this carousel and so the chances are that you will make the same mistakes, errors, misjudgments or act inauthentically again in the future.

The image I get from my environment is they like a puppet, a string puppet, and their mind is making them dance because they made a misjudgment. They made a mistake again and then the human centered mind in the inner child berates them for making the mistake, and then they make it again. They are almost addicted, and they cannot change it because they create this feeling. Then, this is very important, the word you use is guilt. When you use these words: guilt, regret and shame, you have to distinguish what you are describing, is it a feeling or are you giving yourself a belief? Guilt, in my experience, when you say you feel guilty, you believe you are guilty. Then you create a feeling which is uncomfortable and painful. You call that feeling guilt, but the guilt lies in the belief. The belief brings things like, "I did wrong," "I hurt people," "People will never forgive me," "I was such a bad person, I should not have been like this, but I was and so many people have been hurt." All embedded beliefs create the red

…gs (regret, shame, guilt, etc.) which we called guilt, but … …em is in the beliefs. The beliefs are basically you being extremely hard on yourself, demanding and not allowing yourself the opportunity that every human being should have. We do occasionally make mistakes that's the only way we can learn and grow. You are not learning the life lesson, but you are choosing to just constantly berate yourself by having these harsh expectations of the person you should have been. It seems like such a simple step, but I can tell you from my experiences with people, stop saying, "I feel guilty." Own it. "I am guilty." Then I would say, if I was working with you, "What are you guilty of?" Now, I can tell you the majority of people are experiencing the same situation because they are so connected to the feeling of shame, guilt and all the words you said. That's why I do not like these words because they confuse your thinking and that's what the human centered mind in the inner child likes because you are confused.

After pressing the issue, I would ask my clients what they are you guilty of, they would respond, "Well, I am guilty of making a mistake." I'd say, "You should not make mistakes," then they would go quiet again. Well, we all make mistakes but this mistake really hurt somebody. I am sorry but most mistakes will hurt someone else so your responsibility is to go to that person you hurt and to say, "I am sorry that my mistake affected you." What is more important is to find out why you made the justification and the excuses to yourself for coming to that decision. You see, when you ask the three golden questions, it will always come to making the choice and this is what I hear from my clients, "Oh well, it is a habit." No, no, no, no, a habit is just a choice set on default. "Oh, it is my subconscious mind." I am sorry, but your subconscious is over 90% of your mind and you have to OWN it. You have to take responsibility because if you do not own it, this is acceptance. Then, it is very difficult for you to change it because it is not yours to change. You are the victim. Instead of saying, "hands up I really messed up there," let's understand why you messed up and try your best to make it right to the people you may have hurt. They may not accept it, and you have to accept that. You may have overstepped the mark and they will not accept it. It has broken the relationship, and you have to accept that because you cannot make them accept it. You are beating yourself up, you punishing yourself, and that's why the word guilty is so important because I often say to people I work with, "You are guilty of that and making that mistake. Now, what is your sentence?" and they would ask, "What do you mean?" You are punishing yourself aren't you? How long do you punish yourself for? I see, for many people, this is a life sentence. Well What difference is that going to make about the incident if you are punishing yourself for the rest of your life?. It is not going to change that mistake , but somehow our human centered mind convinces us if we punished ourselves through wallowing and torturing ourselves with these red light feelings of regret, shame and guilt, if we just constantly do this, then somehow it will right the wrongs. This is a complete misunderstanding that the spiritual way, the higher self-way, is to reflect on what you have done. Learn the lesson; if you are able to go and speak to the people who are affected, take emotional self-responsibility for facing up to that challenge because it will not be easy. It might be very uncomfortable facing up to their reactions because they may not want to hear you. They may not want to speak to you, and that's the spiritual way. That's the authentic self way to take, so learn the lesson and take self-responsibility. I was once upon a time sitting in the place you are, and I know what you are going through. I have learned my lessons. This is your time to take self-responsibility; own it and accept it. I cannot make you learn the lesson, but, while I learned my lesson, I did stop saying it was not me, I was not wallowing, "It was my parent, it was the school, or it was a teacher." My self-healing journey is not different from your journey, believe me, but I have learned the lesson. I am now sharing this lesson with you, and that's the meaning of this life lesson. It is not good to keep beating yourself. It is not good to keep putting yourself on the carousel of despair. It is not good to have a life sentence because nothing is going to change. It is a difficult pill to swallow, to say, "I was wrong, I really messed up, I really did." Then, to sit back and say, "I am NOT an evil person. I am not a bad person. There was a set of thought processes and circumstances that led to me to making those decisions." If you do not learn this is the life lesson, guess what will happen again? The same thing will happen again and again...

There is a big teaching here, I want you see that. Making a mistake, doing something in your past that may have been extremely wrong or inappropriate does not mean you are a bad person. It is just means your actions, your thoughts and your decisions at the time were inauthentic. It was not mature enough and appropriate. It did hurt people, but it is not about you as a person or what you did. Making that separation is so important because your higher self knows, your authentic or spiritual self knows, that we are divine spiritual beings. No matter what we do in our life journey, it does not affect that authentic beautiful essence of who we are and to almost tell ourselves, and is not different to tell ourselves, that we're a bad person that we're evil, that we're soiled, that we're not worthy or that we're not deserving. It is almost a crime in itself really. The bigger crime is you are making misjudgments, making a mistake, and then you are going on to create even bigger crimes and mistakes; you are not learning the lesson, this why I call these life lessons, and do not get offended because I am not telling you these life lessons are easy. They are very challenging to get your head around, but you have to stop this continuation because carrying on and doing the same thing has no benefit. It is only exacerbates what is going on. You are living your life in these extremes, red light feelings, and it is only more likely you are going to make more different mistakes because you are not connected to your spiritual self.

There must be a payoff or benefit for the human centered mind, the paradigm, the ego or the inner child. It must perceive that there is a benefit or good reason to keep re-experiencing, to keep ruminating, so rather than going back, reflecting, taking the life lesson and moving on; the inner child or subconscious mind wants to keep us stuck on this carousel of despair, rethinking it, ruminating on it and torturing ourselves with it. The inner child believes there is a payoff for doing that. The payoff is very strong because it means you do not take responsibility. The payoff is when things go wrong in your life, you can go quickly and easily and say, "I am a bad person." You say, "I will never get things right. Everything I do goes wrong," and this is the carousel of despair. When I have a talk with people around me, I ask them, "Why are you a bad person? Why are you feeling that way?" They tell me they did something and I say, "Well, that was not a good thing that you did," then they go on and they reinforce the results of the outcome. If you think you are bad person, then the results don't go your way, and you do bad things, then it becomes a self-fulfilling prophecy. Then you can feel sorry for yourself. You can go down and down and down, so it is, in the way, the inner child that becomes familiar and that is your life journey. This is why the life lesson has not been learned.

You are now, instead of living to your higher true self, following your spirit and using your higher self as a compass, under the control of your inner child. The inner child has this self-fulfilling prophecy, but nothing is ever done, everything is a disaster, and everything never works out right for you. There is more proof, there is more proof! The human centered mind in the inner child is not there for you to prosper and expand to be the greatest you can be. It is trying to keep you emotionally safe and keeping you locked in this prison of self-doubt.

Many people have done things in the past that they are not proud of and they cannot resolve it and move on. When they experience happy times in their life, that's when the inner child jumps in, "You do not deserve to be happy because remember what you did," and it wants to drag you back to that dark place. What we need to do is say, "Stop it!" Connect to your spiritual self, your authentic self. Rather than constantly listening to the inner child and keeping us on this familiar self-torturing path where we belief we need to constantly berate ourselves, we need to follow the spiritual path of self-responsibility and take the life lesson. This is sometimes so hard and you do need professional help because it means going in some dark, difficult places and to admit you are not perfect, that you have made mistakes and those mistakes may have hurt someone else, is a really challenging spiritual journey that you have to go on. The outcome of that is a release. It is a release for you to move on and to start to be an inspiration to others and to show them you can change. You are not the victim of what you did many years ago, unless you want to be a victim. This is so important. Do not be trapped. If you are the receiver of the mistake, then that does not define you as well. If you know something happened to you, and the person was not acting authentically or truthfully, this does not define you; it defines them. This is very important. You need to get personal and emotional self-responsibility. We as human beings, I am sorry I wish I could sit here and say, "No, there are only a handful of people who make these terrible mistakes, and they are subculture and you know something is wrong with them," and the fact is each and every human being has and will make mistakes.

There must be the acknowledgement that nobody is perfect, we are not perfect and other people are not perfect. I think, if we can fully grasp that, that will allow us to release the past issues.

I have mentioned previously about going back and speaking the people who are affected. What if we cannot go back and speak to them because they are no longer with us or we cannot get contact with them? What if we go back to speak to them, and they do not want to know what you have to say because they are holding on to the hurt of what you did to them? They are still angry, they are still frustrated, and they are still not willing to accept what you have to say. It is like that for some people. They need that forgiveness from the other person. They need that acceptance from the other person to say, "I understand. It is okay," before they can move on. How do we square that circle or what is going on with that equation? My answer will be, "You are giving your power to someone else." You are saying, "I need them to release me," but you have locked yourself in your prison. It is only you that can release you, and I would say this part of the life lesson is to respect the people you have hurt, and if they do not want to speak to you; make up to you; listen to you, then part of your loving acceptance is to accept that as well. You cannot make someone do what you want them to do because they may be a life lesson you needed to learn because they have a perfect right to tell you to go. You respect that because that's part of the journey. What I am trying to tell you is all about how you deal with yourself; dealing with yourself is understanding other people and respecting their decisions with their life. You may not agree with them, but they did not agree with you either. This is the mutual acceptance and respect to each other. This called integrity. Having integrity is saying, "I accept that we will never be able to discuss this."

This is about you finding your balance; when you learn the lesson, never come back again, and you will be able to move on. Instead of beating yourself up, flip that over to start doing good.

Accepting your life journey, your patterns, your ups and downs, your learning and growth, your mistakes and errors, and learn from them. In the same way, we have to respect ourselves we have to respect others. If it is not part of their life journey at the moment to accept your apology or to want to talk to you, you have to respect that. That is their life journey too.

This is really important. If months, years or decades later they do not want to speak to you, then part of your life journey will be not to speak to them. Do not forget this. We are all human, and we do make mistakes. I wish we did not make mistakes. I know you are sitting there may be saying, "It should not be this way. Wouldn't it be better if we lived in a universe where nobody made a mistake?" Really, I do not know. Who judges what our mistakes. I do not like words like mistake, wrong, etc. because they are judgmental, but when I wrote this chapter I needed to use some of these words, and this is who we are as human beings, that's the message. That is the physical reality we live in. It is not perfect, but everything is in harmony in their condition. The people we rely on, sometimes, they are out of balance and sometimes we are as well. We have to accept that. This is the difference between seeking forgiveness, whether it is forgiving yourself or forgiving others, often that is a very weighted term. It is a very egocentric human centered mind driven term because it implies a full 100% clear resolution, neat and tidy, packaged and forgotten about. Whereas, for me, the word acceptance is a little bit gritty and little bit more grounded in reality. It can be hard to just accept what we did. It can be hard to accept that someone is not going to say, "Oh well, that was okay." Living that reality, that there is no perfect resolution in terms of what our inner child wants. That acceptance is a little bit more gritty, but it is giving you a lasting sense of inner peace because I think seeking ultimate forgiveness is never going to happen. There is never a neat resolution that we are striving for.

I like to use acceptance instead of forgiveness because the word forgiveness is hierarchical. Who am I to forgive you? It is almost like saying, "I would have never made that mistake." Can I really say that? Can I really say, "I forgive you." It is like I am above you and I see you, but now I will forgive you," and that's why I prefer acceptance. Accept what you have done, but do not agree with it! See, this is the difference. "I am not agreeing with it. I never will agree with it, but I accept it in that instance with those circumstances." You have made that judgement. That is what you did and it does not define you. This is the big difference with beating yourself up because you become almost like a mirror of the mistake you made if you keep on being mean. When people I know beat themselves up for years, I know they have not learned the lesson. Some of them don't want to learn the lesson. As I pointed out earlier, they won't admit this, and I am sure I am going to get more feedback on this chapter than the others. It is so hard to accept as human beings that no one is perfect, we have all made mistakes, and we are all liable to make mistakes. That is very difficult to accept, and I know some people who made mistakes, kept beating themselves up, and made the same mistakes. They repeated the mistake to THEMSELVES thinking that it will right the wrong. You cannot the right the wrong by punishing yourself. If you have made a mistake, and you know it is wrong, all you can do is accept it. If the person won't accept that, then you have to learn the lesson and respect the person. This level of acceptance for what you did is learned through life lessons, through a practice of emotional self-discipline, but also compassion to yourself, not labelling yourself as a bad person and I'm not saying you need to talk to yourself all the time. This is the most spiritual things you can do for yourself now

Transgenerational Forgiveness

You are living in a family chain that spans generations and at times it can seem as though you are experiencing the life events of your ancestors by repeating those in your own timeline. Much of the suffering in life can stem from our family's emotions, patterns of behavior, belief systems and habits; as I mentioned previous chapters in detail, they can transfer from generation to generation. These are usually transferred unintentionally and subconsciously. This is referred to as transgenerational transfer or transgenerational transmission. It is possible to release yourself from these patterns and create new beliefs system so you can reclaim your life as your own. Forgiveness is the ultimate and final measure of releasing resentment, anger and events, once forgiven, it becomes a powerless memory that no longer generates feelings of anger, rage, frustration and resentment. Forgiveness is kept in the heart of the forgiver. It is the one single thing that can set you free from anger, resentment and hurt. Unresolved memories can cause chemical reactions in the body, sending out messenger molecules that create fear, panic, physical ailments, chronic pain, and suppression of the immune system. Resolving these emotions and events from the past are a very important part in restoring the balance to the mind, to the body and to the emotions. Transgenerational transfer has been studied in depth with holocaust survivors and their children. Holocaust survivors experienced loss, powerlessness, and helplessness and they feel guilty about the occurrences that happened. There was the thought, "Why was it me (inner child) that survived." Much of this guilt was transferred to their children and grandchildren, and children of the traumatic, dysfunctional parents have higher levels of cortisol which is a stress hormone. This shows the effect of transgenerational transfer, not only on a mind level, but on a genetic level. The conclusion of my idea is genes that change as a result of environmental factors can be passed down to the generations and this is known as transgenerational epigenetics. For example, poverty is an example of a transferred belief system and behaviors that take place from parent to child. The child becomes programmed and imprinted with parents' behaviors of living in poverty and the child grows into an adult that lacks the knowledge and necessary tools to move beyond poverty. Emotions also can be transferred through generations. My point is, as an human, children we experience many things during our childhood besides the body and mind experience; we experience spiritual ancestral transmission.

When a child grows up in a household with a parent who is angry or sad, there is a higher likelihood that the child will take on that emotion. Many people have unresolved issues with their mothers, fathers, grandparents or with their ancestral lineage, and transgenerational forgiveness is a way that allows us to work with patterns of behaviors, belief systems and emotions that have been passed down through generations.

As children, we were very vulnerable. We get hurt very easily. A different look from our father could make us

unhappy. A word from our mother could cause a wound in our heart. As a young child, ,as human we all have a lot of feelings but it's really hard to express our feelings. We try and try expressing ourselves. Sometimes, even if we get courage and find the words, the adults around us can't hear us, don't listen or won't allow us to talk. We go home to ourselves and talk to our inner child, listen to our child, and respond directly to him/her. Maybe you have done this, even though you received love and care from your parents. The child is still there and may be deeply wounded and the child needs a lot of compassion and attention. It would be nice if every day we would take a couple of minutes to sit quietly and practice this meditation with ourselves. It would be very healing and very calming because the little child in us is still alive and needs to be taken care of. With acknowledgment and communication, we can see that child reflecting to us and he/she starts feeling better. If the child feels better, we feel better also, and we start to feel great freedom. That child within us is not just us. Our parents also suffered as children. Even as adults, they often didn't know how to handle their suffering, so they make their children suffer. They were a victim of their own suffering, and then their children became victims of that suffering too. If we're not able to transform the suffering in us, we'll pass it on to our children. Every parent has been a fragile and vulnerable child. My father and I aren't really two separate entities. I am his continuation, so he is inside me. Helping the little boy that is my father in me heals both of us at the same time. Helping the little girl who was my mother and who is still in me, I help her to transform and be free. I'm a continuation of my mother. That little girl who was wounded and suffered so much is alive in me. If I can transform and heal my mother or father inside of me, I will be able to help them outside of me also. This meditation will generate compassion and understanding directed to ourselves and also to our parents as little children. We talk a lot about understanding, but is there any understanding higher than this? When we can smile, we know we're smiling for our mother and father, and liberating our mother and father. If we practice in this way, then all the questions which make people suffer: Who am I ? Did my mother really want me? Did my father really want me? What meaning does my life have? Become meaningless. We don't need to go back to our native land to find our roots. We just need to be in touch with every cell in our body. Our father, mother, and all of our ancestors are present in a very real way in each cell of our body, even in the bacteria. Awakened understanding has been transmitted to us from all generations, all the sentient beings, and also the so-called non-sentient beings. We are both father and child. Sometimes we manifest as father or mother and sometimes we manifest as the child. As soon as the orange fruit is borne, it has orange seeds in it, so it is already a mother or a father.

Your father was a little child before he became a father. As a little boy, he was quite vulnerable. He could get hurt very easily by your grandpa or your grandma, and by other people. So, if sometimes he was rough or difficult, perhaps it was because of how the little boy in him was treated. Perhaps he was wounded as a young child. If you understand that, perhaps you won't get angry at him anymore. You may have compassion for him. If you have a picture of your father at a young age, you can look at this during the meditation. Look at him when he was little child, and breathe in and out and you will see the five year old who is still alive in him, and in you also. When your mother was five years old, she was also vulnerable and fragile. She may have gotten wounded very easily, and she may not have had a teacher or friend who helped her to heal. So the wound and the pain continue in her. That's why sometimes she may have behaved unkindly to you. If you can see your mother as a fragile little young girl, then you can forgive her very easily with compassion. The little girl who was your mother is always alive in her and in you. If you're a young person, it's important to practice to heal the little child in you. Otherwise, if you have children, you'll transmit your wounded child to your children. If you've already transmitted your wounded child to your son or daughter, it's not too late. You have to practice now to heal the little child in you and to help your son or daughter to heal the wounded child that you have transmitted to him or to her. All of us, as parents and children, can practice together and heal the wounded child in us and in our children. This is an urgent practice. If we can succeed in doing this, communication between us and our family will be restored. Mutual understanding will be possible. We are in our children. We have transmitted ourselves entirely to them. Our sons and our daughters are our continuation. Our sons and our daughters are us. And they will carry us far into the future. If we have the time to love our children with compassion and understanding, they will profit from that and make the future better for themselves, their children, and future generations.

I don't know whether you remember anything from your stay

in the womb of your mother. All of us spent about nine months there; that's quite a long time. I suppose some of us may still remember something, some feeling. Did we smile or cry during that time? I believe that all of us had a chance to smile during that nine month stay. When we're happy, there's a natural tendency to smile. I've seen children smile in their sleep. There must be something wonderful in them to smile like that. I believe that most of us still remember the time spent in the wombs of our mothers. We may only have the impression that we were in a completely safe and protected paradise where we didn't have to worry about anything at all. Now we have lost the paradise inside of our mother. Do you think that in the womb of your mother you dreamed from time to time? We hadn't yet seen the sky or the rivers outside. But in our dreams there might have been something. Perhaps while our mother was dreaming, we saw what she saw. If our mother dreamed about something that was not very pleasant and cried out, maybe we cried out too. If our mother smiled, perhaps we smiled also. We and our mother were something like one person, not two. Between ourselves and our mothers there was a physical link through the umbilical cord. Through the umbilical cord, our mothers channeled food, drink, oxygen, everything, including love. That doesn't mean that our fathers didn't channel anything to us during that time. Some of us had a father who knew we were there and who knew to take very good care of our mother so she could take care of us. Some of us had a father who talked to our mother in a loving voice or talked gently to us in our mother's belly, knowing we could hear him.

Our suffering may be the suffering of our father that he has handed down to us as part of our heritage. The suffering that our mother wasn't able to transform, she transmitted to us. With superficial practice, we can only get the kind of stillness, joy, and happiness that are superficial. That kind of practice is not strong or effective enough to transform the big suffering down at the base. Some of us had a mother who talked to us as well when we were still inside of her. Perhaps we heard her and we responded. Probably from time to time our mother forgot we were there. So we'd give a kick to remind her. Our kick is a bell of mindfulness, and when our mother felt it, she could respond like this: "Darling, I know you are there and I am very happy."

When we were born, someone cut the umbilical cord. We cried aloud for the first time. We had to breathe for ourselves. There was a lot of light around. Our mother continued to hold us. Now we were outside our mother, but we were still inside somehow. Our mother embraced us with love. We embraced our mother. Although the cord was no longer there, we were linked to our mother in a very concrete and intimate way This is the realization that we're not a separate self; we're connected to our ancestors and to all living and non-living beings. We are a continuation of the stream of life. Maybe our parents weren't able to appreciate us, but our grandparents and our ancestors wanted us to come into life. The truth is that our grandparents, our ancestors, always wanted us to be their continuation. If we can know this, we will not suffer so much because of our parents' behavior. Sometimes our parents are full of love and sometimes they are full of anger. This love and anger comes not only from them, but from all previous generations. When we can see this, we no longer blame our parents for our suffering.

CHAPTER EIGHT

COMPASSION TO THE INNER CHILD

Grief can be the garden of compassion. If you keep your heart open through everything, your pain can become your greatest ally in your life's search for love and wisdom.

- Rumi

The essence of trauma, which is underneath human dysfunction, addiction, disease, and confusion, is separate from the self, and in order to make them, the inner child part of you and your spiritual essence, as one; you have to look after yourself. If you want to use the analogy of being a parent, you have to become the parent, so you have to start to deal with all of the stuff that's going on in your life and be responsible and accountable. Stop the comparing, criticizing and being judgmental to yourself. Stop looking around and worrying what other people think and say. You have to think about that first. Are you a person who can parent a child and be compassionate? Are you being self-responsible and being accountable for what you think and what you say? Here, the number one thing is your self-talk; self-image. Please do not believe that because it is self-negative talk, the things you say to yourself does not really matter because no one else is listening to that. Your self-talk is your mantra, your affirmations, so be careful what you are affirming inside not outside. When you have self-talk, it is a conservation with the universe which is listening to you and that has a dramatic effect on you. You cannot do this work if you do not get this first stage right by being truthful and honest with yourself, treating yourself with integrity.

The adult part of you, your mind, is making sure that you are balanced, truthful, living authentically, thinking authentically, not lying to yourself and not criticizing yourself, so what you say it is almost like going to parenting night school to make sure that you are 100% balanced in your day to day adult life. It is almost like prep work It is putting your mortgage, putting your emotional house in order, in order to be a good parent as you embark upon this parenting care journey by contacting and communicating with your inner child. The number one thing for that is self-talk. This is where the cracks appear. This is the first bit that goes wrong with self-talk. It should always be truthful with the highest integrity. What you say to yourself you should be able to say out loud now; think about your self-talk. Could you speak that self-talk out loud so other people can hear it? And a lot of people almost create this duality again. What they say to themselves they would not say aloud. If you do not get that first bit right and you want to be a parent, you have to do the work to become a parent. Respect yourself and have high integrity about what you say and what you do. Have a clear intention, but above all you know this is about being self-responsible and being accountable for yourself and for what you think. Take full responsibility, I cannot keep repeating that word enough, and do not look around to blame other people or worry about what they are thinking and saying. Take responsibility for you. That is the first step, please try that. That's going to take you a while. No one expects you to do it quickly but do it with earnest intentions and you will realize just how your self-talk is. Many of us, we have terrible self-talk, before we embark on healing journey, I had the same self-talk you have and I took self-radical responsibility and I am here now still evolving and growing.

The thing I am talking about is being more authentic, more truthful and more balanced. This is really about learning to connect more and amplify the voice of our higher self, our spiritual self, our true essence or whatever you call it. It is because, I guess for many people, for decades in adulthood they have left the energy the voice of the inner child dominate, and they have been pulled around by the inner child. They have ignored this authenticity, this highest soul, this divine energy, of who they are. They have ignored that so this is really what I am talking about. Step one is an exercise in reconnecting to the spiritual essence of you; the authentic part. I know many spiritual teachings have lots to say for this part. If we can reconnect to that spiritual energy, the mother and feminine energy which is the best place to educate, to guide, to nurture and to support the child's energy which is the human energy and the human centered mind energy; the two of them will work together. That spiritual energy is the loving mother that looks after the child with compassion. I love the quote from the French philosopher Pierre Teilhard De Chardin said, "We are not human beings having a spiritual experience. We are spiritual beings having a human experience." We have to choose if we believe we are humans having spiritual experiences or if we are spiritual beings having human experiences. I believe the latter. I believe that we are a spiritual beings, what I call the spiritual essence of you or the higher self, and that's the mother energy. To do this reparenting work, you have to get fit. You have to clear out your deck, you have to brace yourself because the next step I am going to mention is about when you start addressing the child.

The first thing the inner child will do is to test you like any child, and for a long time you have not been listening to the child, you have been ignoring what the child has been saying, so go to the child and say, "Right now, things are going to change." Do you think the child is going say, "Oh okay, that's fine"? The child does not do that, so the first step is to get your house in order. The second step is reparenting; now, you can start to work with a child. Those of you who are reading this and have children, let's just say you let your child stay up late at 11 o' clock at night, you have never said anything to them and they can go to bed whenever they want, they can play computer games in their bedroom, and all of sudden you think would it be good idea if they went to bed at 8 o' clock. Do you think when you say the child's bedtime is 8 o' clock that they would say, "Oh okay, Mom and Dad. That's a great idea, let's go to bed"? No, the child will push back and the second step is re-educating your child. The moment you start to put some compassionate self-discipline, I am not telling you to start beating your child or be harsh with your child because you have already been doing that and it does not work. It just toughens up the child, but you have to start to think about putting some boundaries or some foundations and some training. You have to build trust and mutual respect, and if you cannot have mutual respect, you have not done stage one. When you are a respectful character, you say what you mean and you speak with honesty and integrity. You speak truthfully, so if you say something like that to a child, if you said to your physical child, "Bedtime is 8 o' clock," then 8 o'clock comes and the child has a temper tantrum, you say, "All right, we can stay up for half an hour," then you have lost that integrity. It is the same idea with reparenting yourself. You have to work stages one and two with your inner child. Compassionate self-discipline is working with your child to bring the child and the adult back together. Step two is placing some ground rules for the child. Before, you were letting the child pull you all around the place, so you were emotional energy swinging all over the place, now, you are trying to bring things back into balance by putting down some ground rules. We know this is going to be healthy for you as the parent and the child, then obviously, holistically, this is the oneness of you. The important thing is that you are prepared for the resistance because this is the whole point of the compassionate self-discipline; the child will resist it. He/she will 100% resist the first time you try it. The second time you try, the child will resist, it will find a way out. You will want to avoid it. The child wants to give up or give you all the reasons why he/she should not do what you are suggesting by telling you why it is too difficult, why it is impossible, why it is not going to be helpful and why it would be easier to do another way. Then, you will hear the lies; "You are not good enough," "You cannot cope," "You are not lovable," "You are vulnerable," and more. But you have heard this and this is how the inner child controls you, so that's why you have to do that first bit. You have to be strong because you have to stand up to the child. You are not beating up the child, but you are showing him/her that you are now in control. It is almost like doing groundwork, strengthening and reconnecting your spiritual essence, reconnecting to your authenticity, reconnecting to your intention, and this work is worth it despite the resistance you know you are going to get initially. This is like planting the roots which give you stability, so when you get the push back from the inner child, you can stand firmly rooted and be compassionately firm with the child. Compassionate self-discipline means not giving in because you have two alternatives; it is pretty straight forward, you either do this work or you carry on down the road of going around and around. It will not heal itself. No one else can do it for you, so if you are constantly looking for external validation, external approval, external strokes and love, then this is the problem. You are not taking self-responsibility, and then you stay on the carousel of despair going around and around, "Poor me! I am not good enough. I cannot cope. I am unlovable." Now, the child will want you on that carousel because child likes the familiarity; the child is used to it. The child does not like the unknown. When you start to give something like self-discipline, which was never given it before, the child is going to kick off big time, and this is where you have got to do stage one. Make sure you are ready for this and that you are firm because you will not get it right. Being self-compassionate with yourself, accepting you are not perfect, and you will inevitably not get everything right, not get the inner child to work with you the way you would like it to, is the fear in the first few stages. But, try again the next day because authentically you know you are rooted and grounded in the knowledge that this process is worth it. This second stage can affect your emotions the most. That's why you are engaging with your inner child and bringing them into one. These can affect your emotions the most because your child has a direct connection to your emotions. That's when you will start using words like fearful scared overwhelmed all of these words. That's why completing stage one is the most important. Getting yourself fit to do this first stage is like getting fit and training to run a marathon. This is the marathon now. This is where you and the child have to work hard for maybe two or three weeks, maybe a month, because the child will not give up. We spoke about this many times; one of the qualities of the child is determination. He/she is stubborn. I nearly swore there, but the child is very stubborn and will not give in. The child does not like the unknown and wants to push you down. The child wants you to give up and, in the past, you have always given up. The child thinks if he/she keeps on pushing, you will give up, and you will let him/her have his/her own way. That's why the stage one, doing that training, is very important, so you are totally focused this.

The child really values the known against the unknown, so if you are persistent, strong and unwavering, that becomes the known, and then the child would just accept that because that is now the known. The child knows and has tried all of the tricks in the book for you to give up, but if he/she knows you are strong, the child won't resist. Then, that becomes the known, and the child comes together with the adult part of you. That's the oneness. The inner child created a vow and this vow caused separation. I am talking about the union of you, the inner child part of you and your spiritual essence, coming together as a unit in oneness. The first stage is important getting your training right because this is the stage where the fireworks happen. The child will push against the ground rules. You know the new authentic way of doing things, but the child prefers that to mixed messages, so this is why it is actually good if you are applying the same rules. You may have a lapse, but overall there is a consistent application of the rules and explaining why we are going to do things differently now or why we are going to deal with this person differently now. Then, as you say it, it becomes familiar for the child, but if you are chopping and changing and sometimes revert back to what the child wants, sometimes going into on extreme and going back to the authentic way, those mixed messages only to serve to confuse the child and confuse you. This is the maze of confusion. That's you in the maze now. The child will like that because it is familiar; he/she is not changing. The child really does not want to change even though he/she knows this way is not working; the child values familiarity. If the child can persuade you to go into the maze of confusion, you will be running around the maze, getting lost and the child makes it more and more confusing. This is where I came across many people everywhere. When they are trying to control that part of the mind, the inner child, it starts kicking back. Remember, it is you. It is showing your strength and nothing bad is going to happen here, but you have a choice; you either take control and live your life authentically and truthfully with honesty and integrity, or you keep on playing this game where you are allowing your child to win. This is why you have stage one to get yourself fit, focused and knowledgeable about what you are going to do. Do not make it too harsh, make it loving, caring, compassionate or all of the things I have mentioned, but there has to be a firmness. This is what people get misunderstood about sensitivity. You can do this sensitively, because as long as you are being firm, it does not mean you are not sensitive. Being sensitive means it is your superpower you can do it with sensitivity.

The idea of compassion, rather than just discipline, is communicating ground rules in a way the child can understand, so in a soft way, in a soft but firm way. We are not saying, "You must do this. I am not listening to you. This is for your own good." It is none of that; it is just firm explanations like, "This is a way we are going to do this now, and I am going to look after you. We are going to make sure this is all right, and if you have any concern about that, we will talk about it later." You would appropriately communicate with a child in a way that is sensitive to their needs, it is not harsh, it is not going to scare them and it is not going to box them off absolutely. You are saying to the child "The more you give me a temper tantrum, the less we can talk because I cannot hear you. So if there is anything I am saying that you disagree with them, then we will communicate." You see, that's how you both start coming together. Now you are starting to become a team. You are moving away from the separation, from the duality and you are coming together as one and that's when you get on the first stage, but this is the most fiery stage. The first stage, I think, is the most important to getting yourself fit for this work, watching your self-talk and clearing up your roars. Knowing that, you can do this. And this is the second stage, when you are engaging with this child who has had no discipline, running wild, and now is trying to put some foundational work in there.

Stage three, after a month of long nights, lots of crying and lots of upset, we are a team now. We can go on and do emotional education and address life's problems when life does not go the way that you believe it should or maybe you believe that you are entitled to deal with life's problems or life lessons. That's where you can go to address when things are not fair, when things do not work out the way you wat, when you will realize that you are not in control. The child always will want to be safe and secure, but the child is actually saying to you that e/she is not safe and secure, "I want to be in control of everything around me so nothing adverse can happen to me." We have to teach the child emotional education and teach you both that is not the reality we live in. We do not live in a Utopian Disney world where everything works out exactly how you think it should be where everything is fair, right and proper for you. It does not work out the way that you believe you are entitled for it to be. Life is not like that in reality. Life has twists and turns, and it has this great ability to slap you in the face when you least expect it, and you have to be able to have the education, the emotional education, to deal with those life lessons. That's why I call them life lessons, there is something you are not expecting. There is something that mostly comes out of the blue and slaps you in the face, but there is a lesson there for you to learn.

Acceptance is a great lesson, not accepting that there is something wrong with you, but accepting that life does not work out the way that you expect it to. And also not accepting that what happened to you, often in childhood, which can be quite traumatic or quite horrific. I am not talking about accepting that what happened was okay. It is just accepting that it happened, and how do you then deal with it. The main point is we are accepting that it did happen in the past. Now, what is the lesson you have learned from that? You can take from that, but it equips you when you meet another twist or turn in your life, you can deal with it. You have everything you need. You are awesome, you have every skill that you need to deal with the lessons that come your way. All I am trying to do is to give you the access to these lessons that you already know, and it is about believing in yourself, loving yourself, valuing yourself and using those skills you already have. When I say access that is the spiritual part of us that already knows that acceptance is the truth. It already knows and understands you cannot control everything; all you can do is control within, so our higher self of energy has this deep wisdom, and it is just about reconnecting to that. It is not going off learning new stuff. It is not about going off getting teachers and gurus. It is not about a long-winded process. It is about tapping into that knowledge which you can then communicate once you have the lines of the communication open with the inner child through the self-discipline. Practice communicating, softly and gently, these truths to educate the child who has been locked and who has been stuck emotionally. This child has been looked in a prison lockdown from the childhood experiences which has caused him/her to retreat within, causing the child to say the vow, "It must be me. There is something wrong with me." This caused the child to misunderstand and label himself/herself, "I am not good enough," "I cannot cope," "I cannot manage", and "I am not lovable." It is about educating the child, and the truth is none of that is true. That is why you have the second step. You are a team, then, when you go to address the life lessons, instead of the child shouting, screaming and overpowering your higher self, the spiritual nature can actually resolve and to solve these from a spiritual point of view. Now you are a team and you work together so if the child shouts off, you now are equally strong to be able to deal with these things, learn the lessons, teach the child the lesson, and then you move on. You do not have to do what I had to do or go and live in the Himalayan mountains for many years. You have already got this; you already have this information. This is the your higher self, your spiritual essence, your spirit or whatever you want to call it. I do not particularly like higher self, but you know this is a part of you that you cannot put in a box or a bottle, you cannot show somebody your sprit, but you know you have it. Once you start to connect to it more and stronger, then through all the these ups and downs, you will learn the lessons, then it will absolutely allow you to grow spiritually the amazingness about you. It will absolutely demonstrate itself in every part of your life and this is so important because this is the filter we are talking about. You know, when I talk about the filter that means every part of your life, not only relationships, but your career, your physical life, your parenting skills, your friendships, your health, your wellbeing and your sleep. Though every single part of you, you have to balance everything that goes through the filter. Also, the more you practice getting comfortable with being a parent to yourself, connecting your spirit, which is part of the process, the more you practice compassionate self-discipline, and the more you look within for the lessons so you can emotionally educate your child. With that, this whole process becomes more effortless and easy. At first, you have never taken this reparenting or self-parenting role because you have always expected your parents or other people as you grow up to do it for you, so it will feel a bit clunky and a bit awkward. We will get frustrated with it but the more you do it, the more you will do it with ease. The whole thing will become more enjoyable and you will flourish because it will become more familiar as well.

On a day to day level, we hear the inner child giving us that self-talk, if you are at work or the kids just came from school, you cannot just tell everyone to stop because you all have to go to the toilet and do some emotional education. Of course, you cannot. Sometimes you can, sometimes when you are sitting down quietly, having a cup of tea, then the child starts off and you can do the work straight away. What I would say and, I guess you know what I am going to say, that everybody should be doing 10 or 15 minutes of meditation a day. When I say meditation, I am talking about this work, being focused on controlling your mind. This is the first stage as well before you start the process. I would recommend you get into a habit of 10 to 15 minutes in a day. You can do it when you wake up as the first thing in the morning and the last thing in the night. When you are having a cup of tea, just drop your shoulders, take a breath, then start dealing with the issues the child was giving you previously. In your self-talk, listen to it because there will be lots of work for you to do there to get that straight. If you are experiencing it in the middle of the night and your self-talk, your inner child, is going crazy telling you this and that, then address the issues by sitting down in a quiet meditation, journaling, going for a walk or setting aside the time to listen and address those concerns and give the child the teachings. That's the emotional education but if you have not done stage two, and brining the two parts of you together, the child will not accept the teachings because he/she does not trust you, so that's why we split the process up into three stages. The first one is to get yourself fit, healthy and ready for the "fight". The second one is the wrestling match with the child and the third one is where you both deal with emotional education and life lessons because life will not be the way you wanted to. I am sorry if you are expecting life to pan out the way you think is fair. It will not happen. That's the reality you live in, I live in and we all live in. Life has twists and turns, so things will happen that we do not like, and it is how we deal with them that defines who we are as a person. This defines the oneness of who we are so please if you do not like thought of meditating, try walking or journaling, do not give up if got red light feelings just go over these practices , keep trying it , be easy with yourself because you will find and align the one for you.

CHAPTER NINE

ATTITUDE IS EVERYTHING

"You cannot travel the path until you have become the path itself."

-Buddha

If we change our thinking we change our lives. It does not matter if you grew up in a poor family, if you had an abusive or excessively traumatic childhood, if you had a dysfunctional family and culture or even if you had love from your parents and your loved ones. What matters is the strength and greatness in you and the ability to see this in you. This takes a little work on yourself. I did use affirmations in order to change my attitude towards myself. I do not mean do seven days and stop it. No, you need to do this like eating food and drinking water if want to feed your soul, your spirit and to change your inner child programming. You can do this till you see physical, emotional and mental changes. Just keep doing it. You will see amazing results.

In this world, the people who suffer, the people who have so much negative influences in their life, they did amazing things for humanity. The current condition you live in, does not define you. I want you understand something here. Many of us grow up in the most intense surroundings of negative attitudes that most of us have never expressed in our entire lives which is the evidence, I think, of the fact that there are ways and means of maintaining a positive mental attitude, even though you are surrounded with negative influences. The subject of a positive mental attitude is so important. I want you know that; I want you to get the essence of this chapter.

A positive mental attitude is a state of mind which every person must create and maintain by the method of his/her own choice through the operations of his/her own willpower based on his/her motivation and adoption. Positive mental attitude is based on a defined purpose, activated by a burning desire and intensified until the burning desire is elevated to the plane of applied faith. When it comes to wishes, everyone has a flock of them. When it comes to curiosity, everyone has a full stock of it. When it comes to hope, perhaps half of us have hopes for unattained things or circumstances. Burning desire is only expressed by a small percentage of people who can be called successful. Very few feel the urge of this burning desire. Applied faith is something only the leaders attain because of the degree of mind control which can exist only in a positive mental attitude. Prayers bring positive results when it is expressed in a positive mental attitude. The most effective prayers are those expressed by individuals who have conditioned their minds habitually. Think in terms of mental attitude. For a great number of years, it was a mystery to me as to why my prayers failed more often then they succeeded. When I found out the real cause, I discovered that I was in the habit of going to pray only when I was in difficulty, when I wanted something so badly. Later, I learned that the best way to go pray is to condition the mind long before an emergency arises by expressing thanks and gratitude for the blessings you already have. The vibration thoughts sent out from the person's mind carry with them, through to other minds. The precise state of mind in which they are released, if you learn how to condition your mind before, you will manifest things to your life. After you learned the art of conditioning the mind of your dreams and desires, the positive vibration of the mind goes and affects the minds of others and situations. No one can teach your personal achievement or healing your inner child while in a negative mental attitude. Understand this first. Speakers cannot hold and influence their audience and lawyers cannot convince their jury without the aid of a positive mental attitude, and it has been said that the most successful doctors, in all branches of therapy, are those who treat their patients with a positive mental attitude. If doctors went to sickrooms in a negative mental attitude, there would not be a chance on Earth for them to do their patients any good.

Your subconscious mind or the inner child part of your mind can be educated to produce constructive results only when it is given instructions in a positive mental attitude. The subconscious mind responds most favorably and immediately to a burning desire backed by applied faith. Faith followed by actions. Constructive mottos of affirmations are often used by people who can recognize what a powerful influence one's daily environment has on the makings of a positive mental attitude. I use many hours writing and listening to these affirmations as well. Here is one of them: "You can do it if you can believe in you." How true is that? Whatever you are tackling, whatever part of your life has a problem, rewrite that part again with your words how you want them. You can solve it if you believe you can. The person who is worth most requires the least amount of supervision. And how true that is? Remember your only limitation is that which you set up in your own mind. You fix your own limitations. Nobody can fix them for you. The tone of your voice speaks louder than your words. Keep it pleasing, please. A negative mind spawns only negative ideas. A real master saleswoman will not, under any circumstances, approach a prospective buyer until she has first conditioned her mind to be absolutely positive because she knows the prospective buyers will pick up her own feelings and act upon them. This can apply to any aspect in our lives. Closed minds stumble over the blessings of life without discovering them. If you have a positive mental attitude you attract opportunities you want, favorable opportunities, relationships you want to have, the amount of money you dream of, just like a magnet attracts steel. And in reverse, if you keep repeating the traumas, the experiences you had before will keep repeating. You will attract situations based on the mental attitude you have. What you think you will become. You will repel all opportunities.

A transmutation procedure is very simple, when your paradigm or inner child overtakes, you start thinking of it as it had been a big shift in your paradigm and you healed yourself. Start imagining your circumstances or situations of your inner child as being healed in the way you desire. Start also looking for the seeds of the equivalent benefit which seems to come with every circumstance. While wounds of disappointment and trauma are wide open, it is very difficult for one to start looking for that seed of the equivalent or a greater benefit. But if you allow a little time to pass on after any type of adversity and begin to search, you will find that seed of an equivalent benefit. It never fails; it is always just waiting for you to discover it.

When fears overtake you, just remember that fear is only faith in reverse gear. And start thinking in terms of faith by seeing yourself, translating faith into whatever circumstance or thing you desire. When sorrow overtakes, you start expressing yourself in terms of joy, perhaps by singing or giving thanks for your power to convert sorrow into joy.

Act out these positive parts and they will become real. Is that not an amazing thought? Of course, when you start acting joyously when the people around you know that your heart is burdened with sorrow, you may seem ridiculous but never mind what other people think. It is that what you think that counts.

Have a session with yourself in the bathroom every evening just before sleeping. Look at yourself in the mirror and complement yourself orally and enthusiastically for having already accomplished the things you desire to accomplish tomorrow. And do not stop until you have convinced yourself what you wish to happen tomorrow will happen. You know nature has a way of seeing to it that what you expect comes along. She does not want to disappoint. If you expect failure, if you expect to feel unloved by people, or attracting abusive relationships like your parents, if you expect defeat, if you expect ill health, if you expect feeling the same way or that things will not change, the chances are that you will not be disappointed. But if you expect feeling loved, healthy relationships, feeling free, changing old beliefs, shifting your paradigm, starting a positive life, having good experiences and having amazing people around you who are all far better, the chances are also that you will not be disappointed.

Who is the greatest person living at the present time? My answer is, of course, that you are the greatest person now living in the present. If you do not believe this then begin at once to tell yourself it is true or it is true as far as you are concerned; you do not know any person living past or present or who is more important than you are. Of course, you do not. You are awesome because you can always become what you sincerely desire to be. That might not be true in the place you were born or lived in. But those external things do not define you, they are not criteria for your advancement.

If I were to ask you to think about good friends, the ones you like, and write down what do you like, 95 % of the people will put down attitude as number one. That is how important this attitude is to all of us. And with the proper attitude, we look on in a completely different manner. How wonderful it is to possess such a positive attitude where you get up early in the morning and think about how it is so wonderful to be alive, to thank God, the Universe or whatever you call it, for giving you yet another day to live. You walk out of your house into the garden, take a deep breath and think, "How amazing! Thank you, divine, for the breath I breathe." There is a miracle taking place all around us. Every atom and every molecule of this air is miraculous. You look at the Sun, and once again, you offer your gratitude to cosmic power residing in the Sun who by his miraculous powers is providing us with the sunlight that we need. And then, we go through life with that positive attitude in this manner of thinking the biggest difficulties and hardships never prevent anybody from succeeding. These people are who have been the most successful in human history, despite having so many difficulties in life. Demosthenes was the greatest orator in the western world. In his youth, he used to stutter. Despite that difficulty, his positive attitude carried him forth. Homer, the writer of the greatest Western epics the Iliad and the Odyssey was blind. Julius Caesar was an epileptic. Charles Dickens was lame. Plato, the greatest philosopher of the Western hemisphere, was a hunchback. But these difficulties did not prevent their souls from blossoming. Those who achieved exceptional greatness in their entire life journey, most likely as you and I did, they experienced abuse, a dysfunctional family and environment, excessive hardships that even our minds cannot acquire, but in their long journey, they unleash the greatness in them with this positive attitude to be in service of humanity.

This positive attitude leads joy from within and that kind of joy can never take away from us. So, to make our lives a success, it is important to cultivate the mind. And when the mind is cultivated we naturally operate in a harmonious manner in every part of our life.

How can you make a positive mental attitude work for you? The best way to answer that is to explain how it worked for me and the experiences of many people whom I have meet over the years. How positive thinking works out in your own experience, of course, will be determined by your personality, your own attitudes and your own faith, but first of all think we have to determine what is a positive attitude. There are many definitions. I can start by describing positive thinkers, and I would say positive thinkers are people who see every difficulty and who see them straight without victimizing themselves nor be discouraged by them because they know the exercise of they own inherent strengths. They can meet any situations and overcome any problem. People who have positive thinking or a positive attitude do not have an egotistical attitude, but a substantial attitude of confidence. They are also people who realize the distinction between negative thinking and positive thinking. Negative thinkers do a very dangerous thing. They constantly send out into the world negative thoughts and they activate the world negatively. There is a law known as the Law of Attraction, the light attracts light, so negative thinkers constantly send out negative thoughts and make everything around them negative in nature, and in that very nature, they draw back to themselves negative results. On the other side, positive thinkers send out positive thoughts and they activate the world around them positively. They get positive results.

One thing that I have noticed in the lives of people is that those who affirm that they are going to have positive results seem to attract them. I will share some examples; all my school life I was the top student. The image I was holding in myself helped me to achieve my goals because I had that image in me and I did it with honors, and I had another image of my dream job, I affirmed all my university life, no matter if I had ups and downs in my life, at the end of the period I reached this goal as well. And writing this book was an image in me, I put the seed in my mind, I planted it and with affirmations I started my journey, and you are reading this now. I had a goal, not a fuzzy goal; a sharp, clearly defined goal, and I had the image held in my conscious mind until finally it sank in by process of intellectual osmosis into my subconscious mind. When it got into my unconsciousness, I had it. So I would say one of the most important things about making positive thinking work for you is to have a goal, hold it as an image, and affirm it every day as you consume food and water. Then, give it all you have. Another thing I have discovered about positive thinkers who make positive thinking work for them is that they have a very good opinion of themselves which means they have self-love. They believe that they have something in their nature that can be stepped up. I remember when I was very young, I was a pretty shy backward kind of a girl. I met a teacher in my 3rd year of school who said something to me one day, and I never did forget it nor did I ever forget him. He said to me, "Reyhan, never build a case against yourself," you see, up to that time I had been saying to myself, "I will not amount to anything. I haven't got any brain. I haven't got any great abilities, I am a minority, and I never can get anywhere." I found after a while that people were agreeing with me, and it is true; people will accept you at your own self appraisals. I was constantly building a case against myself, and as a result, I was not doing very well. But when I decided the almighty has given me a normal brain, a normal personality and normal opportunities, I was going to go out and make the most of it. If we were to do all the things we are capable of doing we would literally astound ourselves. Attitude is very vital, in fact.

CHAPTER TEN

POWER OF GRATITUDE

"Gratitude is the wine for the soul. Go on. Get drunk."

- Rumi

"How can I train my brain to think positive?" I can hear you are thinking about how you can think positive and have gratitude if you are afraid and have doubt.

The moment you permit your mind to dwell on dissatisfaction with things as they are, you begin to lose ground. You fix your attention on the common, the ordinary, the negative, the squalid and the mean; your mind takes the form of these things, then you will transmit these forms or mental images to the formless and the common, the negative, the squalid and the mean will come to you.

But the value of gratitude does not consist solely of getting you more blessings in the future. Without gratitude, you can no longer keep from dissatisfied thoughts, regarding things as they are.

The grateful mind is constantly fixed upon the best; therefore, it tends to become the best; it takes the form or character of the best and will receive the best. Also, faith is born from gratitude. The grateful mind continually expects good things and expectations become faith. The reaction of the gratitude upon one's own mind produces faith; an ongoing wave of grateful thanksgiving increases faith. Someone who has no feeling of gratitude can no longer retain a living faith; without a living faith, you cannot get more blessings, joy or happiness by the creative way.

It is necessary, then, to cultivate the attitude of being grateful for every good thing that comes to you and to give thanks continuously. And because all things have contributed to your advancement, you should include all things in your gratitude.

Read this statement carefully:

"Throw your heart over the bar and your body will follow" Norman Vincent Peale states.

Fix this statement in your mind, if you really want to do something with your life, the heart is the center of creative activities. If your gratitude is strong and constant, the reaction in formless substance will be strong and continuous if you follow your heart with burning desire; you will get whatever you want. Your wants always will be towards you. You cannot exercise much power without gratitude for it is gratitude that keeps you connected to power.

Benjamin Franklin said, "Whatever you're waiting for, be of peace of mind, contentment, health. It will surely come; but only when you're ready to receive it with openness and gratitude. Of all the characteristics needed for both a happy and morally decent life, none surpasses gratitude. Happiness and health are the just rewards for living in gratitude."

Does gratitude have power? You might ask power of what? I will explain and define gratitude in order to have a clear understanding. Gratitude has the power to these three things; to heal, to energize and to change lives. In fact, many people do attribute a healing power to gratefulness; it can heal them of past hurts as well as give them hope and inspiration for the future. People say that it can change their lives, it represents, in many cases, a "turning of the mind" to focus not on what one is lacking or deprived of, but which one already has a light, so the definition of gratitude I want to share with you is very short and very simple, but it consists of two components: the first one is the affirmation of goodness. We affirm that there are good things, benefits, gifts and that life is good. It does not mean life is perfect, that there are not some complaints, some burdens, some hassles of living, as we look at our lives as a whole. If we look at life accurately, we can identify a number of good things or some amount of goodness in our life. That's one step; the second step is figuring out where that goodness comes from. We make an attribution, psychologists would say. We make a casual decision or inference about where this good stuff came from. Who do I give thanks to if I am thankful? It almost implies, does not it, a giver behind that gift? There is someone to give thanks to, and so we acknowledge or recognize the sources of this goodness are outside of ourselves. It was not anything we necessarily did ourselves which we might take pride in. Let's say, we are happy or proud of something we did. But in a humble dependence, we acknowledge that other people did things for us or if you are of a spiritual mindset you might attribute that to God, the Universe, a higher power or to a supernatural being. We say that there are other forces that provided this benefit for us, did for us what we could not do for ourselves from which we recognize a dependence and we are grateful for the gift we received. now, there is a distinction between feeling grateful, the short-term feeling, the emotion of gratitude you might feel when you are given a gift. For instance, if someone provides you with a benefit, you feel thankful and that can be a very powerful feeling. I do not want to minimize that one, but there is a difference between that short-term feeling and saying that someone is a grateful person, that they habitually look at life with a graceful focus or through gratitude glasses. That's very different, so we could align levels of gratitude on a continuum from the habit of saying thank you, to a deeper, abiding sense of thankfulness for life as a fundamental life orientation. That's a different degree of gratitude. So, gratitude has a complexity; it has a depth to it. The more you study it and read about it and talk to people, the more you can appreciate that is not as simple as just being appreciative or being thankful. There are many nuances and complexities to gratitude, and we are not creating grateful people through these elements. We want to try, I mean, I think that would be the ultimate goal, to help individuals develop gratitude more as a deeper orientation, as an attitude towards life, just because of those benefits that it seems to provide. What is a grateful person? You might say a grateful person is one who is able to receive gifts that other people are providing for them or see life itself as a gift. The grateful person, at the other extreme end of this continuum of gratefulness, is one who accepts all of life, good and bad. Everything that happens, they see it as a gift or potential gift. Now, it is quite a bit different than journaling all the nice things that are happening to you, but you have to start somewhere. I would not assume that all people find it very easy to keep a journal or even to think in a grateful framework because of some reasons I will talk about shortly. Some of the obstacles to gratitude seem so much easier and so much more automatic and habitual than grateful thinking.

Grateful people have advantages when it comes to success in life; they tend to be happier and tend to be more satisfied, but they also tend to be doing good things as well. It is not just feeling good because gratitude produces positive feelings, but it also leads to doing good; it leads to acts of generosity and compassion. Grateful people are more forgiving; grateful people are more pro-social. They are helping others, and people are saying this about them. It is not just them saying this about themselves. Well, I think that grateful people and ungrateful people have different ways of looking at life. It is very hard to find people who are very ungrateful. In fact, if you look throughout the history of ideas, you see in-gratitude being excoriated as a vice, you know, it is one of the worst things people can say about you that you are an ungrateful person. In some cases, it really represents sociopathy or anti-social behavior because reciprocity is such a universal norm that when people do good things for us, we do good things in return. We do not return harm for good, so it is unusual to find an ungrateful person, but there are ones who are less grateful who have a different orientation towards life for various reasons. They are going to focus more on what life is denying, what they are losing out on, looking at life with a lens of scarcity, paradigms versus a lens of abundance. They are looking at life as a burden, focusing on deprivations and resentments versus life as a gift. Satisfaction, what life is offering, is a very different orientation now because these are extremes and many people fall in between, and even the most grateful people have times where they feel deprived, feel injustices and so forth. They are committed against them. Generally, I am talking about two extremes: there are the most grateful and the least grateful individuals, and I think part of the reason why we see the positive effects of gratitude is because on the left, I have this different orientation looking at oneself, looking at other people, looking at the world-a positive trait-which leads to more functional positive outcomes.

And after all these ideas you start to say, "Well, tell me how I practice it." The most important thing is that you practice mindfulness to be present, be in the moment you are living in. And what is mindfulness? What does mindfulness mean? I think it means being aware of your mind and not letting your mind, your experiences, your paradigms, your inner child, rule over you. It is not letting your mind control you. Everybody thinks mindfulness is a kind of modern self-help, the personal development world think mindfulness is related to meditation practices you can go to a meditation class for. They kind of get confused as to what it is, something of a religious practice. Meditation does not mean sitting cross legged in a dark room for hours and hour and hours. Meditation is also about being in control of the mind; you can have a meditative mind and it does not mean you have to be still or quiet or light candles around us or sit in front of Buddha. You can meditate by just being in control of your mind. We always come back to you are the master of your mind, the mind does not master you. And mindfulness is not going to a meditation class once a week, I am practicing once in an hour and then forgetting about it. It should be part of your daily routine, you should be mindful all of the time, when you are driving, when you are cooking, when you are with your family, when you are at work, you should be mindful of controlling your mind, not letting your mind be doing a double summersault. And a lot of people, they think their mind is somewhere out of them, talking at them, telling them things. That's not the mind. You are not separate from your mind. And mindful practice can remind you about that in an environment so it is something you can go on and practice for yourself. As we are doing this, I am being mindful. I am being mindful to get my message across to make sure I convey this point clearly, and you are being mindful to ask me questions while you are reading this book. So, this is a mindfulness exercise. this is something we do not talk about, and we do not teach our kids, and many do not know as well, about the nature and how the mind works how they should control the mind. I think we teach them that the mind is almost separate from them, it cannot be controlled. To have control over the inner child, you need to master mindfulness to reach the point of oneness, bliss, joy, gratitude. Being in control of your mind and taking responsibility, I call it compassionate self-responsibility or compassionate self-discipline, and not letting the mind go on these journeys. I will give you a couple of scenarios; first one you say, "Well, I am on my commute to work on the train. It is really busy hectic and cramped, and I am already starting to get through one door because my mind is racing ahead, I am thinking about what I have got to do right. I am getting frustrated with people being noisy next to me, pushing into me, so how I can be mindful on that train journey?" My answer will be how about dropping your shoulders, taking a breath and just be thankful. Thankfully you have got a job go to, that hopefully you enjoy, thankful you enjoy the commute, not jumping ahead of what might be, what could be, what should be, just being in the moment, just being in the now, as Eckhart Tolle says, and just create an air around you that you are in control of you, so do not allow yourself to be dragged along. That's exactly what I was saying, the mind control would drag you along and you start to think about what you should be doing and what you could be doing. This is what you have chosen to do. Just be in this moment and enjoy the moment and enjoy again, so do not let your mind have control over you, stop it. Come back and control your mind. Drop your shoulders, you can do it now and everywhere as you are, how you are, just drop your shoulders and take a breath.

So most people want to tap into mindfulness in a situation whereby they would rather get red light feelings of stress, anxiety, etc. But there is also a benefit in being mindful all of the time in more positive situations, that should be the easiest time to be mindful. If you go back to the original thing, whereas when you say I have red light feelings, it means you are not being mindful, you have allowed your mind to pull you, and to rule all over you, such as, cooking, walking, craft work. Well, it's much easier to be mindful because when you are mindful, you are focusing on what you are doing, enjoying and getting pleasure from it. And so therefore, it is much easier to be mindful. And use the green light and red light feelings analogy, green lights are positive and you are aligned, red lights are when you are not aligned, your mind is out of control. Get back into control, right now. Stop it. Control the mind; it is not your enemy; it is not fighting you. It is not all over you. Take compassionate self-discipline. Bring it back into your control and so mindfulness is the practice of clearing your mind, telling your mind and keeping your mind in the present moment, absolutely independent now because this is all we have. We do not have yesterday, it is gone. Tomorrow is not here. We have now. All you can do is right now and keep in this moment. All I can do is pass this message over to you and hope that you will go and practice right now, today, not next week, not next class, not tomorrow. Now, right now. Be mindful of whatever you are going to do next, whether that is sitting down and relaxing and watching tv, cooking dinner. Whatever it is, do it mindfully, do it authentically, do it the best that you can do it. Be the best that you can be. Just be in your space in your energy, do not allow the mind to run away with you. And when you get into that place, in that space, it is wonderful that mindfulness creates an effortless way, whatever you are doing, kind of free time, personal time, enjoying yourself, being with family, at work in a more pressured situation, mindfulness, I think is a technique that can apply to all.

And let me give some examples to you on gratitude, I will tell you a story of mine. When I was little, kids got the bus to school. There was a boy on the bus named Aho, he was mentally handicapped, he had a low IQ, he spoke kind of funny, and the other kids made fun of him. Aho never took offence, at least, it was looking like that. He was so sweet natured. The other kids would not play with him, but I always liked Aho because he was nice and he became my friend, and he taught me some important things: great teachers do not need a big IQ, they need big hearts, and when I think of him, I feel gratitude. One morning, I am late getting ready for school, my brother leaves the house, and I am still pulling my little dress on over my head. I open my underwear drawer and it is empty–I go to the laundry room, grab some underwear from the clean laundry basket, put those on, pull on my socks, lift up my shoes, find my lunch box and begin to run. It is a half-mile to the bus stop down a hill, then around a sharp turn. Before I can even see the bus I hear its horn, toot-toot-toot-toot telling me to run faster, taking that last sharp turn, I look up to see all the kids faces in the bus windows frowning at me for keeping them waiting, and the driver is shaking his head with impatience. I am almost there when I feel something creeping down my legs and I realize that when I grabbed that underwear from the clean laundry basket, I must have gotten my mother's underwear. Hers is white, bright cotton just like mine, only a whole lot bigger, and suddenly, I have to stop running because that bright, white underwear lies wrapped around my feet. I look up and all the kids faces are howling with laughter. I set down my lunch box to reach for the underwear to pull it back on. Pick up my lunch box again, holding the underwear in place and hobble on the bus. Then, what happened, as the bus doors swung open, all that laughter shrank into silence. Not one kid would make eye contact with me, much less let me sit with them, except there in the back was Aho waving at me with one hand and the other patting the seat beside him. Just like I always did, I sat down ready to burst into tears, ashamed, full of self-pity, so sorry for myself. Aho waited quietly until the bus began to move and then he kind of elbowed me and made me a funny face. We both began to laugh, the more we laughed, the less ashamed I felt, and then something truly remarkable happened. My heart was swollen with gratitude for Aho and that was when I was full of gratitude. And I did not just feel ashamed I felt wonderful. Gratitude can take us from feeling sorry for ourselves to feeling joy. Over the decades, it turns out, it is me who is the slow learner because I had to learn gratitude more than once. I think I finally got it. And I want to share with you the full scoop on gratitude.

Doing a daily gratitude exercise will make you happier and

more self-disciplined. More able to achieve your dreams, goals. Even physically healthier and perhaps, best of all, gratitude frees us from emotional pain. If you want to let go of emotional pain, choose gratitude. Or if you simply want to have more joy, choose gratitude because when you feel more joy and you make the world more joyful. You need just three easy keys: emote, extend and exercise. Emote, meaning, it is not enough just to think about gratitude, you have got to feel emotion; extend, as in extend gratitude beyond yourself to include other people, be grateful for other people; exercise, do your daily gratitude exercise as mindfulness... When you practice gratitude correctly you tap into neuroplasticity, brain plasticity, that's the discovery that we can restructure our physical brains by using our minds to create better brain cells, connections. When you use the three keys, you unlock your neuroplasticity. When you emote, you fire up to the hippocampus your brain center of learning and memory When you extend your gratitude to include other people, you spark the most highly evolved areas of the human brain, devoted to social intelligence and finally order for those wonderful new brain cell connections to go into long term memory to spread out into the subconscious, where they become deep beliefs that drive you forward. That takes regular repetition of daily exercise; emote, extend and exercise. Repeat while you are reading these phrases.

Gratitude is especially powerful at healing childhood wounds (inner child), one example is a talented architect who grew up with a cruel abusive father, and he was carrying around a sense of victimhood which was understandable, but it made him feel helpless, have less self-esteem, lack self-love, which was limiting his personal and professional success. Using the three keys, my friend began doing daily gratitude exercises, within one month, he was attracting better customers, making more money. Plus, now he is just a whole lot happier. He called me to say how glad he is just being thankful for the things he has, he wrote, instead of focusing on the things he does not have. All of us experienced some level of negativity, trauma during childhood and that is just life. No one wanted those things to happen to them. The problem is children are vulnerable, children cannot defend themselves, as I mentioned in previous chapters, they do not know how to handle the emotions or situations in their experience. The part of the brain that allows us to make our own judgements and to block red light or harmful information is the prefrontal cortex, right up on your upper forehead. It is the last part of the brain to develop. It is a physical structure that is not fully formed until after 20 years of age, so when we are kids negative information, limited beliefs, traumas, slips easily deep into the brain unfiltered. And the more emotionally charged those negative messages are, the more they stick in the subconscious. They become what I call limiting beliefs, the paradigm, the inner child, which will hold us back just as my friend's sense of victimhood was holding him back... Gratitude freed my friend of all old limiting beliefs. It can do the same for you. I am grateful even for my inner circle history as strange as it was, and I want to share some of that history with you to show you the power of gratitude.

Here is one of the real stories. When my friend was young, her father abandoned her family and her mother, eventually became a radical lesbian, at one point, she told my friend she was no longer her mother. For a little kid to understand this really hard and harsh experience, and the father was a hopeless alcoholic, he showed up for work so many times drunk, got fired from his job, then one afternoon lying on his bed, he passed out drunk with a cigarette in his hand and burned down the house. He and her brother, who was also home at the time, were lucky to get out alive. Her brother was three years older than her, twice as big, became violent during his teenage years and quite dangerous to her, personally. Today, he is classified by the government as a severe paranoid schizophrenic by law. He is on a lot of medication and so on. My point is here, a dysfunctional family affected not only my friend, it affected her brother more than her because he did not have coping mechanisms, he did not know how to handle it, they did not have parents around to help them to pass through together the suffering in their experience. There were many wonderful aspects about her childhood, they lived in the forest with dogs, cats and a pet bunny. That was heaven, but the negative effects of her childhood crept up on her at around age 30 in the form of self-pity and bad behavior. She was destructively acting out, behaving badly, blaming her own behavior on her own family. She was confused, she went to see a shrink, and that time had psychotherapy, but things were getting worse and worse. Finally, in her late 30s, a friend came to help her. Once again, her friend, Dalia, thought her gratitude exercises. Gratitude saved her life. Gratitude has kept her happy ever since. It will do the same for you.

If it is a new thought to you, that gratitude brings your whole mind into closer harmony with the creative energies of the universe, consider it well and you will see that it is true. The good things you already have come to you along the lines of obedience to the certain laws. Gratitude will lead your mind out along the way by which things come; and it will keep you in close harmony with creative thought and prevent you from falling into competitive thought. And gratitude alone will keep you looking forward to the infinite and all, and prevent you from falling into the error of thinking of the beauty, love, blessing, harmony, friendship, success, money as limited; and to do that would be fatal to your hopes and dreams. This is the law of gratitude, and it is necessary that you should observe the law.

So, let us start right to practice gratitude now. If you would please close your eyes, and bring into your mind someone you are grateful for. It could be someone close to you: a parent or child, a friend or a spouse; it could be some you have never met, writing, or art that inspires you, or your future life script or what has happened already. Consider the preciousness of what they have given you. Think about ten things, maybe they are not in your experience, whether it is encouragement, wisdom, love, success, money, the family you want, the house you dream of, just feel it, smell it, sense it with closed eyes. Your dream is already yours as that feeling of gratitude grows stronger within, allow yourself to smile, to smile with deep gratitude, to feel it in your body. Send love to three persons who are bothering you; if you find it challenging to send love to the person who bothers you, get yourself in a state, think about something or someone who makes you happy, and during this, slip the person who bothers you in this picture and fill it with love and send love to all those three persons with deep gratitude. Then, take a minute and ask for guidance and blessings from your spirit for your day. And write it down, this gratitude exercise, before starting your day in the morning and before sleeping.

CHAPTER ELEVEN

HOW TO LOVE YOURSELF: SELF LOVE

"You, yourself, as much as anybody in the entire universe, deserve your love and affection."

- Buddha

Do you love yourself ? Can you love someone if you do not love yourself? Why do we hate ourselves? Why are we struggling to love ourselves? Can you give answers to these questions? Let me dive into these questions and explain why, where and when we start unloving ourselves. Yes, you can love yourself whilst not loving you, but I would ask why are you not loving you? I mean, if you can love someone else truly and not love yourself, does it affect of your ability to or the quality of the love that you give your partner or your husband or anyone in your life? Try to define love; what does it mean for you and you say, "Love is an emotion, as an act giving energy, an ability to love someone or something," well, you are choosing to take that action. My question is here: why are you making the definition on loving someone else? Your partner, your wife and choosing not to love you because, at the end of the day, this a choice you are making. This is a really, really very important point. It goes back to self-nurturing, nurturing yourself, so you are making the choice. Most people will love somebody else and value them, but they choose not to love themselves, and you say, "It is okay for them to receive my love and I want to give them my love, but I do not choose myself." It is the choice you are making, but you would have been making it for a long time. Most people use the word habit, and now, remember, a habit is just a choice that you set on default. So, stop using the word habit and think about choice and why you are choosing to love your partner, but choosing not to love you. Why are you not making this for you? Here is the analogy: let's say, you have a big bowl of delicious cherries and 14 people, and you share it in four servings, and leave none for yourself. Why would you do that to yourself? Why would you bother to do that? This concept of thinking everywhere and in everyone. I did entire my life too. Most of us are stuck on the principle that self-love is selfish. This is one of the main beliefs; this is the way I grew up. I used to have this belief as well as you. This is not a direct thought, but it was indirectly injected into me. You must put others first was a rule of my life; this was what I was taught. And I believe that this is an incorrect teaching. And, I believe that you love yourself so you can love others; it is a flow of energy. You should not be manipulating that flow. Think about it like breastfeeding a child, if you see a mother breastfeeding a child, the first thing the mother does is to be careful about what she is eating and drinking, she needs to nurture herself so she can nurture the child; and if you think about it that way, if you let the love flow through you, then you have enough to flow through to everyone else, so it has to come through you first. Let me get back to the question again, if you are choosing to love someone else and not love yourself, to me, this is going to be a harsh word, but I am going to use it, this is a manipulation. You are not allowing a natural flow of the energy of love to flow through you and out. You are doing a kind of manipulation to get validation from that person for them to love you. So, they make you feel better. Where you should be doing that this is what self-love is for you. In another way to say this, is the human condition, human centered mind, that makes what is a natural cycle and natural flow that you can have. And you can observe everything in every animal, plant, every kind of creature in the universe is part of this flow in this cycle which happens naturally. You see it in the birds, when they are feeding their chicks, but also, they are feeding themselves, so they can look after the chicks. It is only the human centered mind (inner child) or ego is the kind of content that steps in and tries to fiddle around with they are as a manipulator. So, it is a process that it is the mind, human centered mind, the ego, that steps in, and it complicates this matter. Let's go back to the question again, if you love your partner, but choose not to love yourself, and here you need to do a golden thread, why? Why? Why? Why? Ask this question till you reach to the root of the incident or events you have experienced in childhood and this Q and A process will take you down to the three lies to your core beliefs which I have mentioned in previous chapters; I am not good enough, I am not lovable, I cannot cope. So, if you have got any of those lies, you have got to clear those, ask yourself why? And I will say to you; "I disagree with you, you are lovable." I will even go more; "I think you are awesome, prove me wrong. Yeah, prove it, please." And what do you normally get? Somebody says, "Well, I made a mistake." We all make mistakes that does not make you unlovable, so stop it.

If you choose those lies to dictate your thoughts, feelings and actions, then you will start manipulation. The game of the energy of love and how you dole out and know whether you let the love flow through you or push it away from you, and expect others to give it to you. The fact is you are seeking them as a resource, so it is almost like there is a piece of you missing, and you are looking for someone else to put that into you. Most people have this cycle inside, and they say they were not loved by their parents or in their childhood, they were not loved in the way they should have been loved, or their parents had difficulty in loving them. What they are saying is because their parents did not love them or love them the way they should have been loved, now again, they are going to choose to not love them as well. I think the position on that is when I was young, I was made to feel or believe that I was not worthy of love. I believed that lie, now, I am an adult; I am still believing that, therefore, I do not think I am worthy to give myself self-love, so it is almost like this is heart hardwiring or this perception of a hardwiring of the belief and that belief entered into the brain. How do you overcome that? A lot of people will use those to get hardwired. You are not hardwired; you are not thinking about it because somebody told you that they practiced that as a child. I am very sorry, I wish it had not happened, but it did happen to you. If it did happen to you, then do not carry it on. What they did was wrong, incorrect; they should not have done that. Why are you carrying an action that is wrong? It is almost like they pass the baton to you. You do not take the baton, this is when people laugh at me when I was writing this book; it is so important, stop it, stop it now, do not carry it on. It was about teachings. Whatever the reason those parents, carers, teachers, whatever the reason, that was their reason, not your reason. In terms of what their reason was, often, it was because they did not love themselves. It is like a parcel, if you like, a parcel of misunderstanding about how divine, wonderful and lovable you are. It has probably been passed down from generation to the next. Now, this is your chance and to say to yourself that this is enough and you are going to parent yourself, "I'm going to reparent my inner child in a way that I know and is true for an authentic life and loving and what I deserve." The analogy I mentioned, do not take that parcel. It is not going to help you. If you take that parcel, you may pass it on without realizing it to other generations. Teach your children how to love themselves by you loving yourself. We as children learn by example. Nurture yourself, look after yourself, take care of yourself, this is not selfish, this is self-fulfilling this is really giving such a great example to those around you with how you nurture yourself.

And now you think and say, "How I can start to nurture and love myself?" First of all, the emotions from the belief and or the thought that created it, so if we are talking about love and you agree with me, that's emotion. Think about what you have to believe or what you have to think to create the emotion of love. How do you love your partner? What it is that you look for as their greatest assets? You look for what turns you on about them. You look for their good side. That means you need to reflect to your own personal qualities now. I am not talking about practice after, I am not saying well self-love is making sure you go to a yoga class once a week or making sure you eat healthy. I am going to the root of what is it that you really value: yourself. This is why you cannot lie. I can see why because many people would not ask themselves that question, let go, "Well, I am not good enough," and then say, "What? Prove it to me," and I go, "I cannot." Do not do that, when you say you are not perfect, no one's perfect, so look for the best of your qualities and start to love your best qualities. So if you are good at art, if you are a good mother, if you are a good partner, if you are a good provider, start to think about positive sides of you and value that positive side. You do not go looking for the negative side of you. You do not burn yourself with self-talk. Well, you do not do this with your partner. You do not sit down thinking, now, what do I hate about her? What really gets on my nerves? Let's focus on that. So stop it, really stop it. Self-talk can be that cruel, it can be nasty, this is why if someone said, in your friend group, they do not like the word, they do not think the word lying is a harsh word, it is not a harsh word, it is a true word. Be consistent about you, if I am going to tell you that you are not perfect, you will not get everything right. Human beings learn only by making mistakes. Do not focus on your mistakes, use them as lessons to learn to grow, to mature, to be the best that you can be; focus on your success. Focus on the times you have done something brilliant, but if you can do it, pat yourself on your back and say well done. You know you are doing the best thing you can do, and when you make a mistake, think about what you need to learn from this, seek wisdom, seek lessons, do not go and do the same mistake again. So, the case of self-love begins with being honest, truthful and reflecting on your own qualities. Watching your self-talk, learning from your mistakes, learning few mistakes, so many of you out there, you are into your feelings. There, you love your emotions, you want to keep on talking about, "I feel this, I feel that," you know, where I would just use red or green light feelings; if you are getting red light feelings about yourself, you are lying to yourself. I cannot make it more clear than that. And now, stop it, go back to the thought and think about what in these thoughts is the truth. I will tell you, it is a lie. How do you do this yourself? If you want to use your feelings when you think about yourself, create green light feelings; joy, bliss, love, happiness, flow, flourishing. Do that about yourself okay, so take a minute and answer, is it not so much easier to beat yourself up? Stop it, stop it, I cannot be more precise. It is wrong; it is not true; you are awesome. If you do not think you are awesome, ask yourself why you're not. Why aren't you good enough, why aren't you lovable, why can't you cope? Tell me, why you do not value yourself? Sit down and construct that and do not try to say, "Well, I have made mistakes," because we have all made mistakes. There is no small or big mistake; all are relative and IS. And, we all have to make mistakes. And, I know some of us say, "I am so busy looking after my home, looking after the children, cleaning the house, I have not got time for me." So what? You put cleaning the house over you. This is crazy, put some dust on your house, in fact, turn the beam over, go have a bath and enjoy the beam being over in your kitchen. You are making some choices there. Clarify your choices. Get your priorities right. You should be flowing through you. So, you have got time to clean the house, you have got time to dust, switch the radio or music on while you are cooking, you can feed yourself mindfully and nurture yourself.

If you tell me how I can love myself more, I would like to ask you, instead, how you can accept yourself more that the way most of us have been socialized the way in which the child gets to learn the initial learning (inner child or paradigm). The parents are under pressure to socialize the child, make the child socially functional, and doing that, they emotionally, whether they intend to or not, reward and punish the child for behaviors and the result is that when that starts very early, before there is a lot of reasoning process, between the parent and child, the child has certain emotional feelings that certain feelings sits in its natural states are not acceptable, and the result is some feelings of unworthiness or inadequacy or something in most human beings as the result of socialization, very few people ever come through socialization unscathed in some way or another. I mean, that is not an unfair statement. I do not think so, in a way, you could see that your inner child or ego, or your paradigm, is in a way built upon and that's where Sigmund Freud understood it. He saw that the repression of it, or the impulse of life because the way the society has to deal with the child impulses to get it to be socialized, usually the child is left with a feeling that somehow I am bad, I have these things that are not acceptable, and then you build this social structure and often what you end up with is a personality that is constantly looking to the world and other people, "Do you approve of me, do you like me, am I good enough, am I acceptable to you, and have I achieved enough here?" And, you get an A for your effort and you feel good. And if you do not get the A, it is not like you feel nothing, you feel bad, and it is as if the baseline is negative not zero. So, that you are constantly using your life experiences as a way to disprove a basic negative feeling about yourself that is a very common thing in social structures, and in human development in inner child development. Many psychological systems, like Freud's system, for example, work primarily with the negative going to zero. This is the domain that you work with right behind that is where the spiritual dimension begins, and that is a part that looks at the universe and just sees it as it is. It does not sees the art when you have got a negative feelings, the opposite when you trying to undo it, you could undo it by emphasizing the positive like if you do not like yourself, you could emphasize, "I love myself," which how do we love ourselves more is one of the questions of this chapter, or we could say, "Let's go behind love and hate and find a place where we merely acknowledge ourselves, where we just allow our humanity." We hear that there is negativity in us, and there is inadequacy and we allow ourselves, and the word that I have come up with, that I am finding as the most comfortable word to work with, is the word appreciation. We kind of just update what is interesting. The way I have looked at it is that you go out into the woods, into the forest, and you look at trees and you appreciate the trees. Do not say that tree is good, that the tree is bad because one tree is fat, one tree is thin, or one is tall and one is short, or one is bent and one is straight, unless you are in the lumber business, for the most part. You just look at the trees and you appreciate them the way they are. They are what they are, you can appreciate them, but the minute you get near humans, it is interesting that you immediately go into a judging mode. You come into better and worse. And you do that out of your own insecurities. You do that out of your own need, constantly to be reassuring yourself. So you say that person has got more hair than I do. You go and directly find dimensions, constantly judging and equating, am I as good, am I equal to, am I as good as a mother, am I as beautiful as a woman, whatever it is, whatever dimensions, and you get caught in constantly living in a judging realm, and if you start to practice seeing people as trees, I do mean in the sense of appreciating them, who they are. Including yourself. It's just starting to appreciate yourself. Appreciate your humanity. When you get like, "I am supposed to be this and that and I have worked on myself, I am clear, loving, present, compassionate, accepting. Oftentimes, I get tired, I am angry, I am petulant, I am closed down, now, for a long time, I get into those states," I would really feel embarrassed because that is not the real you, how you are supposed to be, so you would appear like "I was warm, charming, compassionate, and I would dare to be devious and have deception involved, and then I have realized that is bad business because that cuts us off from each other, and I had to risk my truth. I had to risk being human with other people and realized that what we offer each other is our truth and our truth includes all of our stuff, and the first thing I had to accept was my own truth. I had to allow myself to be a human being." That is the point I want to tell, just allow yourself to be human. When you allow that flow, things will start changing through you and in you. Things will fall away so quickly. Many people are locked in the model which is based on negativity, dislike of yourself; when you just allow that you are human with all the foibles, things start to flow and you could feel change occurring in you, and then you can start to experience your own beauty as well as others. It will frighten you because it is so dissonant and discrepant from the model (paradigm) you have cultivated of yourself over the years that you had to do good in order to be beautiful, and the idea that when you look at the tree or a rock or a river, it is in its own way beautiful, you look at decay, it is awesome. You will begin to expand your awareness to be able to look at the universe as it is and see what is called the horrible beauty of it. The horrible and the beauty in all of it because this decay and all of it, I mean we are all decaying, when you look at old people's hand and it is decaying and it is beautiful and horrible at the same moment. Just live with that and then you will start to see the beauty in it. So what we are talking about is appreciating what is not loving yourself as opposed to not liking yourself, but allowing yourself and as you allow, it changes. Love flows through you and to you.

So, you can only love another person to the degree that you love yourself and another person can only love you to the degree that they love themselves. So, if you go through life feeling you are unlovable that will always affect the quality of relationships you have. And if you date or marry or live with someone who thinks they are unlovable, it is very hard to have a really healthy, great relationship. If the person you are with feels unlovable or you at some deep level think that you are unlovable, and more problems occur from people attracting the wrong relationships, staying in the wrong relationships because they feel they are unlovable. But everything changes when you know that you are lovable and you see lovability is essential to being happy. And I have many people who say, "Well, I have never felt love, being in love is just a foreign country to me, I do not know what love is. I have gone through my whole life never having had love," see if you cannot love yourself, nothing really matters. If you take a little kitten or puppy at home, it will run up to you and wrap itself around your legs and jump on your lap because it too thinks, "Hey, I am just this cutest puppy, I am the sweetest little kitten, look how lovable I am." Of course, if you treated it badly, it eventually thinks, "Oh, maybe I am not lovely. These people hit me, they kick me," and it will hide behind the fridge and not come out because we are all born knowing with the unshakable conviction that we are lovable, and things happen (inner child, paradigm) in the early childhood ages that we begin to believe that we are not lovable enough and, sometimes, that we are not lovable at all. And the things that happen are the people who raised us start to say things like "Well, why can't you be like your sister? She is so good. Why can't you be like your brother, he is so tidy or neat?" or "Why can't you be like your cousin, she eats all her food and she is not messy," and we come home with report cards, and our parents say "Well, why couldn't you get A? Your sister got an A." And if you get an A, "Why couldn't you get an A plus?" And when parents do that, they start to label children: this is the good one, this is the smart one, this the pretty one. When you label people, you limit them even when you say to children, "I love you so much because you are beautiful, I love you so much because you are clever," what the child hears is, "Oh, that's why you love me, and if I was not clever or beautiful, maybe you would not love me." And I see many parents say to their babies, "I love you so much, Mommy loves you so much, you will never ever find anyone that loves you like I love you." And after, I would hear parents say it a lot, I had to say, "Look I do not want to interfere here, but I have women who come in my office, who come in and they go back to their date going, 'Nobody will love you like, Daddy, I love you so much. You will never ever find anyone that loves you like I do,' and you are programming your child to believe they will never again find that love." And it is better to say, "I love you so much, because you are so lovable. All your life, you are going to find people who love you like I love you because you are lovable," a very simple adjustment, but that simple adjustment changes. So you were born, I was born, everyone was born, believing, knowing and feeling they are lovable. A baby wakes up and thinks, "Well, it is 4 am but I really think I would like some attention now or some milk or a hug." It does not occur to them. They should not wake up the whole house because they feel lovable, they do not limit themselves, still not programming no paradigm in this stage. We are all born knowing we are lovable. It is very easy to make children feel they are not lovable, "Look at what you did. You are a bad person. You are a naughty person. You did this, you did that," and children take it all onboard because, here is the truth, when you are a baby, you must idealize your parents. We know from the minute we are born that our success, our ability to survive on the planet, is linked to one thing, do our parents love us? If they love us, we will survive and if they do not, we might not. As an analogy, if you look at someone who loves others but does not love herself and who was abandoned by both parents at such an early age, she will always feel unlovable. Princess Diana whose mother left her when she was six years old always felt unlovable. Everyone loved Diana, except for Diana. Once your parents or mother leaves children then say, "But if my own mother could leave, how I can be lovable?" And you know this, we start to have these beliefs and you say, "My mother did not love me because... I did not feel loved because they have preferred my brother, my sister. My mother left, my father left," and we are very fragile when we are very little and we need to feel loved and lovable. If we do not, we blame ourselves. It is too scary to think, "Well, my Mum does not love me she is an alcoholic, my Dad does not love me, he has got bipolar depression." What children say is, "Oh I am not lovable, that's why my mother does not love me. Why doesn't my father hug me? It is my fault, and now I am going to try so hard to be better. I am going to be smarter, nicer, kinder, prettier, and then they will love me," but because it is not your fault, no matter what you do, it does not change anything because the inner child in you has the wrong belief, regardless of appearances. And eventually those people buy into what I call the unspeakable truth, "Oh I guess I am just not lovable, and we go through life and try to find love, trying to make people love us and it really does not work. When you have a sign on your head saying, "Please love me," it actually makes people reject you. When your sign says, "I love me, and I know I am lovable, and I can have a loving relationship with you," then people treat you differently because you have to love yourself first. You have to really love who you are, know you are lovable, believe you are lovable and feel you are lovable, and then your life will change dramatically.

CHAPTER TWELVE

WHAT IS TRUE LOVE?

"Your task is not to seek for love, but merely to seek and find all the barriers within yourself that you have built against it."

- Rumi

All of us ask ourselves what love really truly means, but I am sure very few of us have a deep understanding on love and practice it in our lives, in that sense, I would like to put a glimpse of a different view on love. Because understanding true love starts with ourselves, truly loving yourself and having a deep understanding of yourself without separating from anything and anyone. So true love is something that helps you to suffer less and helps the other person to suffer less. True love is something that makes you happy, and it makes the other person happy. True love can help you to have more freedom, free you from all limitations and help you to be your authentic self, be you.

I think that there are four elements for rendering true love. The first element is "loving kindness"; it means friendship. Loving kindness has the power to offer happiness. When you love someone, you offer your friendship, your brotherhood. When you are able to generate a feeling of joy and happiness to yourself, that is true love offered to yourself, and if you can generate a feeling of joy and happiness to help another person to generate a feeling of joy and happiness, that is loving kindness; that is true love. So, if you are a true lover you can generate happiness for you and for him or for her. And according to the teaching, it is not so difficult to create joy and happiness, just breathe in and recognize the many conditions of happiness and joy that are already available, generating joy and happiness for you and for other persons.

Every one of us has an idea of what happiness is. We are committed to that idea, and if I cannot get this and that, then happiness will not be possible. So, you describe your happiness, you have an idea of your happiness and you are striving to arrive at that, such as a young person falls in love with someone else and in her passion, attachment, she could not see more than that person. She said that person is the only reason why she has to be alive. Her reason is that if she cannot marry that person, she would rather be dead because happiness cannot be possible without that person beside her. And her idea is to get him or to die. For those of us who have not been into that situation, we are able to see that happiness can come from every direction. Happiness can come from West, East, North, South, above and below; and if we are committed to the one idea of happiness, we block all the other avenues; we drop all the venues. Happiness knocks on your door, "Please open, I am happiness," and you say, "No, you are not happiness," and you refuse it because you are already committed to one idea of happiness. And many young people commit suicide because they cannot marry the person they love. In the history of love, there are plenty of things like that and those of us who are free see that happiness can come from everywhere at every moment, the sunshine or the water can bring happiness. A half-hour of walking leisurely can bring happiness, having a cup of tea with a friend or teacher can bring happiness. Happiness can be there every moment of our lives. Why do we have to commit ourselves to just one idea of happiness? Joy and happiness are born from the practice of releasing and letting go. The first thing we need to let go of is our "idea" of happiness, if we are able to let it go, our idea of happiness, happiness will come very easily. If you are not happy, it may be because you are holding on very hard to your idea of happiness. If your beloved one is not happy because you keep imposing your idea of your happiness on him or her; it is very clear and very simple.

The second element of true love is compassion that is the capacity to make yourself suffer less and help the other person suffer less. The compassion is capacity to understand the suffering; to help and remove it. We have learned that there is an art of suffering. If we know how to suffer, we suffer much, much less. And we can make good of suffering in order to cultivate understanding and love. And you can help the other person to suffer less to transform suffering in her or in him. That is the second element of true love: compassion. The Buddha, Jesus, and many holy masters and enlightened beings are able to help people to suffer less because of their great compassion. As we continue to practice, our compassion continues to grow. One day, we will be free from all suffering; it will be great compassion.

The capacity to listen deeply with compassion has to be cultivated. If you are a friend, you should be able to listen to your friend with compassion and deeply in order to be really a true friend. If you are a parent, you should be able to listen with compassion deeply with your child and you should transform yourself to be a compassionate deep listener. Because without deep listening, without compassionate listening, there will be no communication and in many cases we live, we love, we truly love and wish the other person to be happy, but we are not able to listen without the capacity to listen deeply. We cannot understand and without understanding, love is not real; love is not possible.

And love is something born from the ground of understanding. You cannot love unless you understand, and this is easy to understand. A husband that does not understand his wife, how could he love her? A wife does not understand her husband if she does not understand the difficulties, the despair, the hopes of her husband. How could she love him? That is why the practice of a wife is to listen deeply with compassion with no prejudices in order to understand her husband. And if the father does not understand the son, or the daughter, does not know what kind of difficulties his son is undergoing, how could that father love his son? That is why it is so clear and so simple to see that understanding is the ground of love. You cannot say that you love him or her unless you understand him or her, and understanding is not something that just happens like that; you have to practice listening deeply in order to really understand. You have to be able to let go of your ideas, your prejudices, because you may already have an idea of how that person can be happy, and you want to import the idea on him or her and by doing so you make him or her suffer, even though you continue to believe that you love him or her. You may be very sincere, you maybe have a lot of love within yourself, but that is not love yet, that is the intention to love, that willingness to love and make one person happy is not love yet. In order to truly love, you have to understand and that is why if you love someone, you should try to understand him or her deeply. You will say understand what? Understand the difficulties that person has, the kind of suffering that person has within himself or herself. The kind of deep hope, deep desire that person has within himself or herself, the kind of obstacles that person is encountering in his or her daily life, you have to see all of that, and if you do not see anything, how could you see everything? You can see a lot but not everything. You should ask him or her, you should go and say, "Darling, do you think I understand you enough?" We need to start this first within ourselves, asking ourselves first. And then you, he and she will tell you, if you ask with all your heart; "Darling, do you think I understand you enough?" You can ask the question to your partner, to your father, to your mother, to your inner child, to your daughter, to your son, and if it is a real question that is asked with all your being, with compassion and with nurturing from your safe place, then that person will tell you and help you to understand. You will not continue to do or to say things that will make him and her suffer. You will help him or her to overcome the difficulties and that is true love. True love is come from understanding the compassionate line cannot be setup by the telephone company alone. You all have to pay something and they will set up a line but that does not mean that with a telephone you can communicate. Now, the telephone is everywhere, you can pick up one everywhere in your city, and yet with the telephone in your hand you cannot communicate. And, in order to communicate, you have to be free of your beliefs, opinions, views, your judgements, you have to be free from your prejudices. And then with the absence of prejudices and judgment you have the opportunity to look deeply and to see reality in itself. The reality in the other person because you declared you love him, you love her or yourself, but you do not really understand him, her or yourself. You have to practice looking deeply by yourself, and you can ask that person to help you understand, and that is the practice of love. You might think that it is the other person that you have who does not understand because the fact remains that you have not understood yourself. You do not know enough about yourself, you do not understand the nature of your own suffering, you have not understood the difficulties that you are going through, you do not understand the nature of your difficulties, the root of your difficulties and your desires. You are in a difficult situation and because you do not understand you, your own situation. And you do not understand yourself, you continue to be caught in a situation, and you do not even want to get out of that situation. When we are caught in a situation, you might think that situation is normal and you do not see yourself in that situation and that is why you do not have the desire to get out of the situation, unless, someone takes you to a far away place and helps you to look back at your situation and see that it is not the situation you want it to be in. And that is a kind on enlightenment. And if you do not have the desire to get out of the situation, you will never get out of it, that is why the first thing you do is have a desire to get out of the situation. You get desire only by leaving that place and going to a far away place and looking back and now you see that this is not a good situation. You and your beloved are caught because both of you suffer deeply every day. First of all, there should be a desire to get out of it and if you are the first one to get out, you will able to help the other person to taste the freedom of love.

And the third element of true love is joy. If love does not generate joy; it is not love. If love makes the other person cry every day, it is not love. If love makes you suffer every day, that is not true love. True love is capable of generating joy for yourself and for other person.

And the fourth element of true love is inclusiveness, nondiscrimination. In true love, you do not see any frontier between the one who loves and the one who is loved-between them there is no frontier. That's why the communication is perfect in true love. Your suffering is her suffering. Your happiness is her happiness. There is no individual suffering or happiness anymore. No discrimination, all inclusive. This is the fourth element of love. You begin with yourself and the other person, but if you continue with this practice of true love, your heart will open, grow and very soon, you will include all of us in your love. You do not exclude anyone anything from your love that is the love of Buddha. I have truly fallen in love with this teaching and I am practicing it. I got so much benefit from it. You are including every living being, not excluding anyone. No discrimination about race, citizenship, religion or anything, and that is the element of non-discrimination.

That is the element of inclusiveness that makes you very, very free, very happy and makes your love unlimited. In true love, you continue to grow. Your love continues to grow, until it embraces everyone in the cosmos.

CHAPTER THIRTEEN

HOW TO BECOME AUTENTIC SELF

"I want to sing like the birds sing, not worrying who listens or what they think."

- Rumi

How can you be yourself? How can you be your authentic self? How do you stay authentic, despite challenges that you may encounter in your life? Most of us tend to label ourselves as a good person or bad. What is it to be a good or bad person? I do not prefer this idea of being a good or a bad person because that is judgmental and, you know, do not compare, do not criticize and do not be judgmental; these are three pillars of being authentic. So when you start to say people are good or bad as you are during a judgment, and so someone is being judged and someone is judging, and so you have created what I call a hierarchical position and that's against the oneness. We are all one pure spiritual being; this is against my teaching, my dharma. We are all connected we are all going through this journey together and who are we to criticize or to say someone's good or bad.

How do you live your life ? What are the standards ? What do you stand for ? And that really is what I think about is one of the underpinning things of being authentic. If you ask me how I know when I meet authentic people or how do I know what an authentic life is like, what does an authentic person look like? Two questions there, so they talk about how do you know you are being authentic, live your truth, do not lie to yourself and you know when you are lying to yourself because you get the red light feelings, so how do you know you are being authentic? You would never compromise yourself. You never compromise what you believe in, make something better for something else or someone else. How do you know somebody else is being authentic? I think we can always sense it. Very important for relationships, look at the word relationships, the ability to relate whether they are friendships, whether they are marriages or whether they are family, and so if you are relating honestly with the truth that is an authentic relationship. You always know when somebody's giving something that is not true. You know they do not really mean it. They are just saying that to you. Whatever you call that intuition or inner guide or gut feeling that gives us inner knowing; it is a sixth sense, your spirit, your authentic self, knows that is true or not. If you can live your life following that spotlight of truth and honesty, then what you do is attract people who are doing the same, and you repel people who are not doing the same because somebody who is not telling you the truth will not want to be with you. If you keep on spotting it, they will have their own red lights and they will become uncomfortable. You will get green light feelings for you because green light feelings are equal, you are tapping into your authenticity. I am saying here that your feelings are very important, interpret your feelings. So you go back to the belief that's created this feeling so you know somewhere in you, if someone is not telling you the truth, you know it already...

And here is an important question, how do I know I am being authentic compared to say just settling for okay? If I use the idea that, you know, you will get strong green light feelings if you are being authentic whether it is a strong sense of calm, a strong sense of an excitement, a strong sense of love or bliss, you know, all those things on that spectrum. What if you are only getting them in a kind of a weak signal, and you do not really get the sense that you do not get passionate about anything does that mean you are not being authentic or is that just the way you are? So, remember I use the idea of the red and green light feelings as a good way to describe your feelings rather than using words like stress and anxiety because that gets confusing, but think of the amber light. And the amber light, it is almost like a set of traffic lights, the amber light is just muddling along. You are not making the decision. You are just going along. This is really a state where you do not want to be. Because who's guiding the boat. You are trying to please people, implicate people, you are worrying about upsetting them, you are worrying about their feelings and so you are compromising yourself and you lose your sense of direction and this, to me, I cannot emphasize how important this is. This goes back to a very, very, very important teaching, my translation of this the spiritual contract and when we come into this world, we come with the contract and this contract has three clauses or three blessings: the number one is intention. So is your intention to muddle along and not really bother and could not care and or be disturbed by making sure everyone else is getting on okay and is happy but you are not? So, is that your intention? And if it is, ask yourself would I teach this to my child, would I say to my child, "You know just muddle along, do not worry, it does not matter just please people," and of course you would not, then why are you doing it for yourself? You know already, stop it. You know this. Do not look for something else to not make excuses. Do not turn your head. Your intention, what your life purpose is, you know, I cannot tell you, no one else can tell you, parents cannot tell you, your partner cannot tell you, but you know. So that's number one, number two, the blessings, all the clauses, truth, honesty and having integrity. Again, this really comes back to this idea of being authentic, do not sell yourself short, do not give up on yourself, do not think it is easier to compromise, do not compromise! I mean this is almost like the death of your authenticity by a thousand little courses. Every time you make a tiny little compromise or sacrifice your truth and what you believe in just because it is a little bit easier and it is no big deal for you. But it is a big deal though! That's the teaching, every little chip away and you are belittling yourself or compromising yourself to please others because you are worried about their feelings or what they think or what they think of you. You are taking a little chip away from you; you must stop it. This is so important and it happens subtly that sometimes you do not even realize that you are doing it. So you have got to be aware of this because this really affects your authentic self. So number one, get your intentions clear, make sure it is a good intention that you would want to pass on to your child or anyone around you. Number two, truth, honesty and integrity. Number three, self-responsibility. Stop comparing yourself with others, stop criticizing yourself and stop being judgmental because this will absolutely chip away at your authenticity because you will become an expert at self-criticizing. You will become an expert at looking over your shoulder and comparing yourself all the time, and when you do that, you put a glass ceiling on your life. And you are looking at other people and you are trying to be better than them or not as good as them. This gets you confused and loses your intention.

On the point of self-responsibility, we would also include under that not blaming other people, not making excuses for not living your truth, not avoiding because maybe for you, it is uncomfortable sometimes to face up to people, and you say "I really want to speak my truth, but I do not want to hurt that person." Here is my answer to this: do you think that person you are so concerned about really does not want to hear your truth? Do you really want to lie to them, and you really think that's better for them? If you are doing this for them, I do not think you are helping them at all. Of course, you do not have to speak your truth harshly, you need to act in certain way. You do not have to purposely upset them. You are a sensitive person surely. You can practice to speak your truth with sensitivity, with integrity and with honesty, and to be honest, I am sorry to say this, if that person, whoever that is, a friend, a partner, a work colleague, if they do not want to hear your truth, you have got to question whether you should have a relationship with this person. And with this point, if it is someone that you cannot get away from, like a person who is a family member, in this point, my answer will be I try my best yet to be sensitive, I would try my best to pick the time. I am not saying you have got to come out and give it to them straight away. You might think, "Well, I just have a cup of tea or I speak with them later on next week." But I would never, never, never under no circumstances would I ever compromise my truth. In my relationships, if someone asked me something, and I thought it might upset that person, I might think, "Well, I will not tell him or her that now while we are in that situation, but I can tell that person all because I do not think I am doing that person any favors. I think I am harming him or her to be honest. It must come from trust. At the end of the day, it is harming the energy of the relationships, so relationships with your partner, your parent, friend, work colleague. It is absolutely about speaking your truth.

Ever since I was a child, as quite a sensitive person, I am quite intuitive, I can tap into what people are feeling or thinking, and I have always kind of modeled myself to be like a mirror of people to fit in, and the problem is over time this has become habitual and in my very early adulthood ages, I started to ask myself "Who am I, I do not know what the authentic me is because I am so used to kind of adapting to different people in different situations to fit in. I do not know whether I am living the authentic me." And what I did is in this point I stopped it, stopped trying to please other people. It was not working, and it does not work and do not use the excuse and the justification: it is a habit. A habit is just a choice that you are making, and you have set it on default. Do not say it is ingrained. It is just a choice that you have set on default. You are making choices. Every time you think something you are making choices. If you are like me, that I was in my early 20s, I have just explained it, or you have been living your life trying to please everybody trying to get them to like you. Can I ask you something? Has it ever worked, is it working now? If it is working now, carry on doing it. You should be happy in the world. You should be full of life with green lights all the time as you scurry around trying to please everybody else in sacrifice of your own life. Loving yourself, allowing the energy to flow through you. First and out is the greatest gift that you can do for you and for those people in your family who you love, your colleagues and your friends. Being truthful so they can rely on you. So, they know that when you say something you absolutely mean it. It is your truth, and they can come back and challenge or you disagree with you and you can go into a debate. I cannot emphasize how this is people talk about confidence. Confidence is a feeling so building confidence is a green light feeling, and being truthful will build those green light feelings. Ducking and diving, placating, half-truths, quarter truths, white lies, all of this stuff is just knocking the confidence down. This will give you amber lights and red lights. You will go down and down and down. It never works. Please be gentle and just go quietly with yourself, is it working? If it is working you would not be reading this book or this chapter or you say, "She does not know what she is talking about. I am really happy to give up on my authenticity. I am really happy pleasing the rest of the universe." Your job is to absolutely nourish yourself. Your job is to flourish. Your job is to give a real inspirational example to your children, your family and your friends to be the best version of yourself. So you can guide them and they will follow you. This is authenticity. Some people might moan and groan, but you will win them over if you do it with love, care and passion. Have a passion about your life. You are divine. Please never, never, never undersell yourself.

People-pleasing is only manipulation. You are manipulating other people to like you. Know that if they do not like you, get them out of your life. It creates space for other people to come in who love you. Why would you fill up your life with people who do not like you, do not even half like you. Let them go find somebody else they like or even like the real you.

Surely the reality is that we live in a society, in a community, whereby we all have to live by a certain set of rules in order to get by. Surely, that is going to involve some sort of compromise of my authenticity. Can we ever be a hundred percent authentic when I am living in the real world? We cannot be a hundred percent anything because that's perfect, and we are not perfect in that sense. And that's why we are like the river flowing down moving and flowing from left to right, but we can really hold on to our authenticity to the highest possible level. I see this as light that I am there I am going towards, so if I use the analogy of the stream or the river, it comes from mountains. It makes its way to the sea, but it does not go directly to it. It flows and finds a way. So I have always got my eye on being truthful, being authentic and having integrity. As I said there might be times if I say something to someone and they are really upset and crying, and you do not say, "And another thing, while I am getting all of this off my chest... " Because that's not being authentic you can be compassionate. Here is the other teaching, flexibility to be authentic is to be flexible to show some sort of resilience and ability to transform and be appropriate. When strong winds come, the bamboo will bend in the wind and flow in the wind. The trees that lose their branches are the big oak trees. They are solid and do not move. The plants that do not lose are the ones that been flexible. So, this is the idea of having this authenticity because everybody is sensitive. You might be less sensitive than me. I might be less sensitive than somebody and so why being authentic is so important. You take personal responsibility for you. Listen to your feelings but do not compromise your self-worth to please other people, to compromise your self-worth to manipulate a situation, do not worry about what other people are feeling, do not purposely go ahead and hurt them. Of course, not. That is not even the case and you may want to keep your gunpowder dry for a day or two and then you say it at the more appropriate time. So if you have got something to say perhaps to a parent, you do not go bang, bang, bang and here is some more. You say what you have got to say and you will keep your gun powder dry, and perhaps next week you bring it up again and you go over this subject. And you say, "Remember a couple of weeks ago, there was another point to bring up here," and you get into this idea that you can debate and you can listen to their point of view as well and they can disagree with you, and you can disagree with them. If you believe something then say it with passion but also be prepared this is what I am always saying myself. If you are disagree all I ever want to is give me the evidence. The evidence, why do you think I am wrong? Why, for instance, do you think it is good to spend your life pleasing people? If you think that's how it should be, then perhaps I am wrong, then give me the reason why. Tell me why I should spend my life pleasing other people?

And I think there is an important point I want to touch here is about being humble, humbleness, humility, let me explain where that fits in to being authentic. It is fitting in really tremendously because when I am speaking my truth to you I am NOT saying, "I am right; you are wrong," what I am saying is I believe this to be right. Please answer what you think. You are good enough to read this book which you are. If you disagree with something that somebody says, "I am worried what other people think of me." If that's the case, you are denying the truth because of a belief that you do not want to show yourself off or upset people and that's wrong. But if you are authentic, there are ways to be more passive, to be more than an observer, this is great as well. If you are trying your best to do things as best as you can in the way that feels right for you. This gives you green light feelings, that's all you can do. And you know you are not perfect. And I like the idea of using your feelings as like a compass and every time you have to make a decision or important choice, what is important or not important at all. It all adds up. It is almost like using your feelings as a compass to guide you, and here with this person or situation or issue, what is the authentic way and check back with your feelings with every step almost. And there is always going to be challenges and conundrums and dilemmas. So, let's say you do something because you write for the magazines, and you submitted to the editor and editor says you tried your best, you have done the best you could do, you said you enjoyed it while writing it, and the editor says, "I am sorry we cannot accept it." So how are you going to handle it? Here is the situation. They have obviously got an idea in their mind of what their authentic truth is for this piece of article. And your authentic truth is from what you have given them, and it does not match. So, you actually did not give a second thought because you know you have done your best. So interesting for that, I want you to consider is when you said you enjoyed writing the article, so enjoy doing what you are doing and then accept it. Acceptance is not that easy and really just let it go. Accept what you did enjoy doing it, you did it to the best of your ability, Maybe it was not right for them just accept them. Wish them love and carry on, put out into the universe, whatever the universe wants to do is up to it, and just move on. As long as you are absolutely content and humble, knowing that you have tried your best. You have enjoyed it. You have done what you can do and then you pass it over to the universe, you know it just might not be the right time. It just might not be the right person or it just might not be, but as long as you keep on sending that good energy, pure and absolutely authentic, then this will come back and that applies to every aspect of your life. So it is not just about caressed or for work stuff, relationships, family stuff, your health, what you do in your spare time, what you do with your friends, everything really. I work with several people who say this to me, "Yes, but it does not happen when I wanted it to happen." You have got to move away from that because that's your expectation. That's you thinking this because you have done something right or good seeing this why these words are really bad. Just because you have done it to the best of your ability, then it should happen at the time that you wanted it to, and this is not the way universe works and this is why acceptance is important. The only question is for you authentically whatever you are doing; you are working whether you are a mother, whether you are a husband, whether you are a friend, whether you are a sport, just do the best that you can do to the highest level that you can do it. Do not be the best in the world, do not compare yourself!!! Just keep on thinking, could I have done it better? Could I have done it quicker? But it is not in a way that fosters self-doubt. And that's where humility comes in. You value yourself, is this something I can learn from? Because remember, these are spiritual lessons that you are learning, but do not criticize yourself. More genuinely interested, am I flourishing and you said I enjoy doing the article because it did not go to the magazine, so what? You have got an article here and you might use it again.

So the last thing to touch upon which kind of leads nicely from what I have mentioned is self-compassion and self-love is essential to opening yourself. These are statements we all say and hear in our daily life, here is one, "I find it very easy to look after other people, but not to look after myself." Have you ever heard this statement, or have you ever said that statement? Think about that statement, it does not make sense, what you are saying is you have value for all the other people; you think you are good enough to care for them, but why do you not care for you? You have to make a difference, separation. This does not make sense. The energy has to flow through you remember the analogy of a breastfeeding mother. She looks after what she eats and drinks so the milk she gives to her baby is of the best quality and that's what we should be doing as human beings. We should be really nurturing ourselves so we flourish, and the energy that we give out is of the best quality. How do you think you are even capable of caring for other people, if you cannot do the number one thing which is to care for yourself? And when I said all these teaching to one of my friends, she said to me, "All is well and good, but is that not being selfish?" No wonder I have got to dedicate my life to this teaching. You know how you can caring for yourself so you can care for other people. It is a cycle of energy through me first, and so I can give to others. So you are connecting to the source, it comes through you, and now this is the basis of the meditation you receive, and remember with breathing, you receive in to let go. You just trust and you will allow breath to enter and flow. And this is what you should be doing with your life force, and if you devalue yourself, you are stopping that natural flow. I tried to explain to my friend for hours and hours because she is operating from a belief, a core belief, what I call a lie, that she is not worthy of giving herself love, so it is that belief like the other lies; I am not good enough, I cannot cope, I am unlovable. It is those core beliefs, lies and misunderstandings which stop you from living, and then how can you be authentic, if you are living in the lie? They do not realize it. Stop it, come to your truth; be truthful now which takes a little practice on how you deliver your truth because you are a sensitive, compassionate loving and caring person. This is who you are, your personal birthright. So what you have got to do is to use those skills of being compassionate, caring, loving, and deliver your truth in a loving way, but make sure it is the truth, do not compromise your truth. Do not give up on your self-worth to please other people do not do that.

Connecting With Your Spiritual Essence

Do you believe there is something beyond your physical body or your mind? Perhaps you are wondering if there more to life than the 3rd dimension or material world or material needs. Are you interested in exploring and understanding your spiritual nature, but in a way that is not necessarily religious or belongs to any belief system? Before explaining these questions, firstly, I need to give you a clear definition on spirituality. I found it very strange that we have so many words about our mind; we call it ego, inner child, but what do I actually mean by spirituality is good feelings, intuition, higher self, inner self, inner knowing, essence, some people like to call the soul or spirit, but is it not interesting how we got all of these words and labels, and do any of them really grasp it? That's why I prefer to use the words spirit or essence. What is your spirit? Something I cannot hold, and I cannot give you a bottle of my spirit, you cannot give me a bucket of your spirit. One of the best ways that I sometimes describe it, if you think of someone you really love, a child, a parent, a sister, a brother and just think of them for a moment in your mind's eye, just picture them the way you see them physically, the color of their hair, their eyes, the way they walk and talk and dress, but is that all they are to you? Just sitting here now, just close your eyes and picture them and I think they have got something more, something that you cannot grasp, but you know it about them and when you are with them you can almost touch it and be aware of it and that's what I would call the spiritual essence or spirit.

Finding balance between your physical self and your spiritual essence, which is a nonphysical side of you, is very fundamental for our wellbeing and finding our true nature and path in this life. As I said, as human beings we are physical so our mind and our body we have our physical energy or physical Qi, but we are also spirit; we are spiritual beings.

The physical side of you is what you can touch, what you can feel, what you can see; the yin, the nonphysical, is this essence, the spirit, this whoever this power is, and I believe and practice that it is perhaps really the fundamental teaching of this book understanding to get the whole spiritual nature that you have. In fact, you know when I talk about red light feelings and emotions, anxiety, depression and all of that, are what I call spiritual disturbance and imbalance in your spirit. So your spirit, higher self, is being disturbed. You are not connecting to your spirit properly. And what the red lights are telling you in that moment when you get a red light, whatever you want to call it, you are not connecting to your spirit; you are connecting more to your physical part, and I think that is an important point because when I say spiritual disturbance what I am not talking about is your spirit is being negatively impacted or damaged or destroyed by something that's happening to you in your life either you are doing it or someone else doing it. Because your spirit, the teaching is, your spirit cannot be damaged, it cannot be destroyed. It is always there, but it is disturbed because we are too much in human energy, and we're too much in our minds. We're too much in the material world. And we also layer blocks, so it is almost like a beautiful candle. If you want to use that expression that never goes out, here comes another teaching: it is we come from a source, we will go back to the source, we are the source. You have got this defined divine energy inside of you there. I caution, but it can never go away. No one ever can touch it, so if this apples to you and you came through a dysfunctional childhood, abusive childhood, they cannot touch your spirit. No one can physically touch your sprit, the only person that can disturb your sprit by blocking, is you, and that is when I talk about life lessons. It is clearing those blocks away so your spiritual essence can come through it. It is always pure. It is never diminished. It has never been affected; it is always there. It is whether you have the trust, whether you have the confidence or the knowledge to touch back to that sprit. This is why I say this is a spiritual teaching that when you are out of balance and experiencing red light feelings, that's telling me when I am working with you that your spirit is disturbed. Our job is to find out what is disturbing it. That's why we dig into reason and we ask why, why, why, and find the blocks and misunderstandings, the lies I call it, but just tell yourself you know the three lies; I am not good enough, I am not lovable, I cannot cope. This cannot be true because you are blocking this divine energy that's within you all this time. In some ways, you are denying yourself, you are denying, your true worth, you are punishing yourself when you say those three lies and live your life based on those lies. You are denying and shutting down one of the greatest most inspirational, I love that word so much, in-spirational, I read it as "in sprit", should you not be living your life in spirit? This is where you have this spark of intuition. You see all these wonderful words this is when whatever comes in your life, in your way, you have the creative imagination to find your way around it. You have this amazing spirit, you have it, no one can take it away from you, and it will be with you all of your life. The question is: are you using it correctly?

All of the teachings in this book are really spiritually based, but I spend most of my time pointing at the inner child being out of balance. Experiencing extremely uncomfortable or painful red light feelings, and I focus on that because they are the things the human centered mind, the core beliefs or self-talk, they are the things that stop us from living in a connected way that's connected to our divine spiritual nature. Our divine spiritual nature is always there, but all of the stuff that goes on in our head can tip us out of balance which means that we ignore and we do not connect to this spiritual essence that we embody. We have this super power within us that could be and should be guiding our lives. So our spiritual essence is like the mother energy or the parent energy to the child energy, which is the human. So this spiritual essence here is another analogy, imagine like you are the captain of your ship you have got the ship, the engines, the physical thing you are going about. You are heading toward your destination, but your compass is the sprit. It is the spiritual direction in your flow. So you should always be referring back to that inner knowing. I said many times in this book, many times, you always know that it is right, using your mental faculties, you will resist yourself and you will fool yourself and you will lie to yourself. This is biggest harm to self-sabotage yourself. Because you are denying one of those most powerful, wonderful parts of who you really are. Yes, you are physical the way you look, the way you act, the way you breathe of yourself, your body that's where you line so that's really important to look after how you exercise and how you eat. How you sleep and what you think is vitally important, but equally, it is important in my view is this nonphysical part of you, whatever you want to call it, whatever you are comfortable with: your intuition, your gut feeling, your inspiration, your inner knowing, your inner knowledge, you always know. How many times, how many times have you said to yourself, "I knew I should not have done that. I knew that was the wrong decision. Something inside of me told me," that's what I am talking about that inner knowing and just connecting back to that so your physical and your nonphysical are more balanced because what I am saying is please tap into this spiritual essence, this spiritual energy, this inner knowing, inner wisdom within you because that is an excellent guide for important life decisions in how to deal with important life challenges, but equally I am not saying we should be living 100% in sprit or following our gut feeling without further question or interrogation, so it is this merging of the two, so merging of the logical mind and thinking, and our experiences in our life today, which obviously factor into our considerations, but equally being informed and inspired and guided by our sprit. So the appropriate balance between those two energies so often I talked about the pendulum that you do not win. You could think about the pendulum again. You should not be too far away. You should not be too far in that way. What I find is most of the time, we are totally in this way, and we are trying to keep ourselves safe and protected. How can we keep ourselves safe and protected from our greatest source of inspiration, and we are cutting that out and what disturbs the spirit. That's what creates red lights because that's when you are not being authentic and truthful that's when you are not on your right path. This is your right path or in the center; you will not get it perfect. You are not perfect you will make those slight adjustments as things come into your life, life lessons you learn. I would say when you are encountering a life lesson that is where you need to be more aware of that spiritual essence, compass, that is telling you even though things are going in the wrong direction, you will be made redundant, a relationship is broken up, there is a death to loved one, that's when you should really be able to connect more to that spiritual side of you because that spirit side of you has a wider perception of everything around you, not just focus down on the next thing. "I should not have done that, they are nasty, look what they are doing," This is the mind really focusing down and the spirit will open it up. And I think there is ego, the human centered mind, that inner child, that part of all our mind does that to spirit, does think, "Well, I cannot prove this, I cannot touch this, I cannot lie, I cannot rely on this, I do not know this for sure." So there, you always got to be mindful of that internal resistance from your mind that says "Until I know something's for sure on that, until I know known outcomes, I cannot trust this part of me," and so for those of us who have not practiced or are not really attuned to or connected to their spiritual self, spiritual energy, their higher self, there is a gradual, almost like getting to know each other period, well, I would say reintroduction because I believe that when you see children. They are connected to that intuition they do things intuitively. They have imaginary friends, and you see a child playing and they are creating these imaginary scenes, and they are very much created, connected to that creative side of them. I think as we go older as we get all get these fears passed onto us by our parents or by school: you cannot do this , you must not do this, do that. You have got to be careful of this. The mind wants to be more and more in control. The mind is wanting to know what is going to happen and to be in control of that, but unfortunately we do not live in that Universe. We live in a Universe of the Unknown, and as you move more in the pendulum to this wanting or wanting to be safe, wanting to be sure, wanting to know, you move away, more away, from the unknown, from inspiration, from allowing things to come into your life by experiencing new experiences, seizing opportunities that we would normally mentally and emotionally close doors on. And then we touch very much on the law of attraction. You see, because when you are going around, I call it the carousel of despair, just on the known, "Well, this is not working, but I kind of know it is not going to work but I know everything." We miss out on all of the opportunities that lie in the law of attraction in the unknown. We should embrace the unknown because this is where your development, this is where your true spirit, your true self will flourish, then one of the things about this teaching is for you to flourish for you to be the best that you can be. How can you be the best that you can be when you are just stuck on the unknown comparing, criticizing, being judgmental about yourself and other people? You are just like a hamster on the wheel going round and round and your energy is becoming more and more and more depleted, rather that sailing off into the unknown, and exploring the unknown and trusting in yourself. You will you have coped with everything; I know your inner child will say you cannot cope. It is all too much. You have always coped to your every situation. No matter how bad, you have been through it, and you have always coped. How dare you even question yourself now? Why do not you set off into that unknown and connect to your spirit and live in your authenticity?

If we connect our spiritual side and find the balance between our human energy and spiritual energy in our daily life, then not only our inner world would be a richer, more abundant experience, but so too is our outer world more exciting, more fulfilling and more flourishing because you are pushing the boundaries back. You are living how a human being should live. Thank goodness someone like Columbus did not want to go off in the unknown as we would have never found America. You know we have as human beings, we have to try, we have to push our boundaries back. We cannot keep on going around these answers where you are denying yourself. You are not living to your full potential, and I want you to live your full potential.

As I told when we are children or when we are born, we innately have this spiritual connection, we are not doubting, we are not overanalyzing, we have not got fears which push us away from our sprit, but that's the truth and because as we grow old into our teenage years and into our adult years, the inner child analyzes over things, compares, criticizes, judges our need for consuming, and building our material world or material safety becomes more important, so we lose the connection to our sprit. So, essentially, what I am telling you now is a reawakening or reconnection to something that's already within us. There always been there it will never go away, and this is very important. If you have had a difficult childhood and I have people around me who said they have been soiled or the have been damaged or they will never be the same again, and this is why this spirit, higher self, teaching is so important. Because I have to try my best to convince them. It does not matter what happened to them physically or emotionally, no one can touch that candle light of spirit that is still shining brightly, even you cannot doubt it. What you can do is to cover it up to disconnect from it. That is the spiritual disturbance when you disconnect from it. And in all of the teachings in this book, I focus because I think that's more effective, on the inner child and how you deal with the inner child and all the lies the inner child tells you and what inner child is trying to achieve. Remember, the inner child is not your enemy. It is trying to achieve the unachievable. Your inner child is trying to keep you safe emotionally which is nonsense because you create the emotions and that's why it never works, so we focus on that but we should never forget our spiritual side because your spirit is there waiting for us to welcome us back into our correct path. You will never be on your authentic way when you are ignoring this inspirational intuitive, good feeling side of you. You can never because you are on some kind of a circle round and round trying to prove something, trying to be better than other people, trying to live in this material world. Now, we do have to live in this material world, I am talking about the style that you live in this material world. We are not denying the material world, we are not denying that you live in the material things where people tell you must have a new car, you must have a new house, you must be slim, you must be fatter, you must have new clothes and more and more. But you have to be connected to the spirit all of this time or you cannot be discerning. You cannot make authentic judgements if you are denying this part of you. So what I am telling is we are allowing the human centered mind to run our lives. We cannot make authentic decisions, judgments, choices, about anything whether it is our career, relationships, friendships money matters, what is our passion, purpose, so right from big high-level stuff down to the meet-my-new-type-of-everyday.

The point is that this spirit is already within us. It is not something that has to be given to us by a guru or God or by studying really, really hard for years or by going to live on top of a mountain or by meditating all day long or by any form of suffering or sacrifice that would be my message. This is something you already have. If you like this expression, it is your gift, it is your gift from the cosmos, from the universe, whatever you call it. It is not something you have to earn or somebody else gives to you. This is why this teaching is non-religious. You, me, we all have it, everyone has it. This is the oneness I keep talking about. When you deny your spirit, the only person that's really suffering is you. You are denying yourself; you are not using a fantastic power, it is hard to give it a name. A fantastic energy that you have got. You are denying it because, "Oh well, I want to be sure, I want to be protected. Oh, I do not want to be hurt. Oh, I am worried about what other people think about me," you see it pales into insignificance. "I am worried about what other people think about me," when you have this immense universal power inside of you, what does it matter what other people think about you? See, when I say to you what other people think of you is none of your business, what is more important is what you think of you, and what you think about how awesome you are, how amazing you are, and you have to stop this nonsense because you have just fallen into a trap and this trap is like a comfort blanket. It is very familiar to you, but you have to be careful of comfort blankets because they can also stifle you and they can keep you trapped down. Do not fall for it and if you are digging that hole, worrying about what other people think, trying to be better than them, tying to have a better car or trying to have a better life. You are on the treadmill and that will just end up with you being exhausted and self-sabotaging, and it is like a vortex, I call it the carousel of despair, that always ends in despair, some kind of despair. Either you are saying something about yourself that is wrong; "I am not good enough, I cannot cope, I am unlovable or I am so tired, I cannot get out bed, I cannot leave. You do not understand Reyhan, I wake up at 3 o'clock in the morning, I have got no energy." There is an abundance of energy that connects to the abundance of the universe.

The spirit, spiritual energy is essentially the energy that connects all of us. The human energy, my physical body, my mind and my brain belongs to me, but the spiritual energy is also mine, but it is part of the collective energy. So we are part of it and that is why that's saying we come from the source, we go back to the source; we are the source. We are all connected. You are connected from my understanding. What I teach to everything trees, flowers, the universe, and within without. We are same thing with everything this is oneness, there is no separation. How can you be better or worse? How can you be not good enough now? Do you want to be superior? How could you be perfect? You see, when you start to really look all these ideas, that the inner child or human centered mind gives you, they are all nonsensical, they do not stand up to any kind of deeper thought, but we live our lives because it is very familiar and we get used to it and we fall into a trap that somehow even the concept. Please take a moment and just drop your shoulders, how could you be emotionally safe when you create the emotion? You create the emotion. How can you be a safe from something that you create? If you do not like the emotion, guess what? Do not create it!!! Stop it! Live in your flow, you are amazing, you are awesome and if you do not think you are, then write down and tell me what it is about you that is not awesome. Do not write, "Well, I am not perfect," because what is perfect? Who judges perfect? You go to this hierarchical value of what is better than what here. They are better than me, they have a better car look at them, they do more than me, I am doing less than them. Oh my goodness! Think about how much energy you waste, throwing it away. And this idea of striving to be something better than divineness that we already are, but do not appreciate what you have, but you can also equally go out of balance by striving for false perfection in terms of being spiritually awakened or spiritually attuned. You know there is no religion, God or guru in all these teachings, if there is, you are the God inside and out. And so is everyone else. So again, it is about getting the human centered mind, the inner child, out the way to allow you to recognize that truth, that fact, and then your life will flow, then your life will be in abundance.

Now I will touch on something many of people have asked themselves, this idea of oneness, as I said, this is about reconnecting or awakening, whatever you want to call it, but most of people in the community says "I am not sure whether I have had a spiritual awakening, all of a sudden I am like viewing the world completely differently from how I viewed my life up to date." I will explain this from my experience, it happened to me. After I have met with my twin flame at that time. It happened one day out of the blue, and I knew it happened; I knew my life would change, but I could never explain. It was almost like it went beyond words for me. I tried my best to explain it, so other could get an idea because I think everybody's reconnection is unique to them, actually, I was looking a bit crazy to people around me because their logical mind could not grasp it, what I was talking about to the people around me. The long story short; I had a spiritual awakening, a near death experience... then I went in deep spiritual seeking the catalyst was my twin flame. Beside of him I get guidance from spiritually ascended masters, angels, ancestors, yoga practices, long hours of meditations, reiki to shamanic healing, crystals, different healing modalities, gurus, healers, books and more and more. All helped me support me to be the person who I am. The experience I had was beyond words and it still is. It is like we are living our life with a torch, a flashlight, we are in a completely black room, dark, and we cannot see anything, except through the beam of this torch, and we live our life through this torch and as we go through this torch beam becomes narrower and narrower and narrower, until it is like a pinprick. I can see you but I could not see anything else around it. And one day, I was in a meditation and going through the teachings and talking to myself the way I talked here. Quite firmly, quite strongly and then something happened, and this was like someone switched the lights on, and all of a sudden I could see everything. I was not the same person and the one moments before. I could see everything, my perception opened up wide and instead of being judgmental, instead of worrying about the dramas I have faced, I was beyond words in bliss. It is hard really to put into words and explain it. There was deep gratitude, joy and bliss from my top to my toes. There was nothing bothering me anymore. All of a sudden it just opened up. I saw people in a different way, I saw myself in a totally different way. I was not so judgmental, I was not so critical of myself, I was not so critical of all of other people. I started to see beauty in everything and everywhere, my diet has changed suddenly and drastically and to be healthy and mindful. I started to have a strong body mind connection. The light switch has stayed on since that date. It stayed with me, but you have to do a bit work because we are living in a universe that keeps on wanting to shut you down, so have you had this when you have said something like "Oh the pennies dropped"? It is same type of thing, not probably so big as I am talking about or I have just had a light bulb moment, and it is like I see. Then once you have that light bulb moment, then you have to work at it. Now, you have to top everything else from clouding you.

And it is this reconnection or awakening to who you are, and I think during our lives we get so much rubbish laid on top of what we cannot do; what we should not do; what they are doing there; you have not passed your exam; you have got to do this; you go in this crew; you have got to that all of these things that you must have and what you must not do, I think these are layers on top of your spirit, and doing the practice, and this is why I share this experiences and teaching with you. I am not telling you what to do; I am saying that I truly, truly believe you are awesome. Now, you prove me wrong.

If I go back to my spiritual journey and how I relate to the spirit, it is completely different from maybe most of you; and I think for the next person, it will be completely different. And again, that's another important point, no one's journey or state of connection is the same. No one is better or worse, again, we do not get into being judgmental, comparing, but I always had an inner kind of inkling that there was something more. I was always naturally drawn to the word that would be esoteric or alternative or spiritual things and from my childhood I am a very highly sensitive person, the way today they labeled as the intuitive empath I am. And I do not know whether that has a connection to it, I am still on my journey, I definitely have to do the work every day to keep my human centered mind from going out of balance, but I do believe I am leading a spiritually connected life now, and I am really happy with it. And I know my spiritual connection to life now will be different next year. It will be different in 10 years' time because I know it is a growing and evolving journey, and I find that really exciting. We do not step into the unknown, and once you say, "Well, I have reached it. I am perfect," then you are absolutely the furthest away. You have more work to do on yourself if you say so. If you start this journey, your spiritual journey, your inner knowing, the universe will guide you along the way to where you are meant to go and where you are meant to be.

CHAPTER FOURTEEN

PROGRAMMING YOUR INNER CHILD, YOUR MIND

"Whatever words we utter should be chosen with care."

- Buddha

This is the bigger monkey wrench in our system, and that is we had started off with the fundamental belief that the conscious and subconscious were just unity of a single mind, so if the conscious mind became aware of something, then the subconscious mind should of course follow along it as well because they are both together. It is two separate minds, but they learn different ways this the critical part. The conscious mind, being creative, can learn in a creative fashion. The conscious mind can read self-help books and after one reading go, "Oh yeah, I have been educated and I know this is how I should do it. This way, my life could be really good if I understood this," and then you say, "Well, I just read the book and I understand how it all works in my life." It is still exactly same, you can go to the lecture, you can read the book you can watch the video, you can even just go aha and the conscious mind, being creative, can learn just from simply reading the book learned. What about the subconscious, which I refer to as the inner child of us? Yeah, here is the problem, it is a habit mind, well, how do we create a habit? I got up reading the book once; it is not a habit so what is the point of a self-help book you read that was picked up information-wise, educated and enhanced your conscious awareness, and yet did not touch any of your subconscious programs, inner child or paradigm. You have the same behavior you had before you read the book, after you read the book. Why is this? The conscious mind learns by reading the book, and the subconscious habit, you do not learn from that one reading of the book. So the conscious mind and subconscious mind learn different ways. How can I teach the subconscious mind? Number one, so many of us talk to ourselves, you know, I love sleeping. That is most lazy discipline, sleeping till 7-8 am. Of course, I had goals and I wanted to wake up at 4-5 am. But my programing was sleeping 8 hours, and it is unhealthy to have less than 8 hours of sleep. You will have an unproductive day. Do not wake up at 5 am, do not wake up early, and then sure enough I slept, I did wake up, but I continue to sleep again. My paradigm programing was so strong and dominating my higher faculties. Then, I woke up at 7 am with being so upset, because even I could do not discipline my mind. How come I can be successful in other parts of my life. I kept talking to myself every morning. Why I did not wake up early? What is ruling over my mind? Here is the fun answer, our inner child programming. The conscious mind, you are in it. That is seed of your identity, your spirit, your consciousness, that's where you are, and you will say who will sent in the subconscious mind ago. Nobody, there is nobody in it. It is a machine like a CD recorder. Why is that relevant? Let's say, I record a program on a CD, put in the machine, push play and place the program, and I say I do not like that program so I say, "Okay CD player, change the program make something more fun and I would like it to be better than this program." Then, of course, the program continues to play just as it was and then you get a little more upset. "Please change that program, wake up early, do you not remember I said to wake up early?" And then, I get so frustrated, very upset with myself, really almost give up because of how many times so I have to tell myself to wake up early, but still end up waking up at 7 am and realize it is not making any difference at all. The point about this, when your conscious mind is telling your subconscious mind not to wake up late, you were expecting to hear that message, and then you realize nobody is in the subconscious like a machine. So I say, "Go talk to the CD player, it is playing a track on an album," and I say "Okay, tell it to play something different. Just talk to it." And the answer is not going to change. They will never change. And I go out there and that is your problem, trying to talk yourself into a change is not going to work because the subconscious mind has nobody to listen to your story. So I asked, how does it change, how does it learn? And here are the three things that can rewrite your subconscious mind and heal your inner child. Number one is how did it learn in the first 7-9 years, the programmable period. The brain was in a low vibrational frequency called Theta. which is hypnosis. So if I use hypnosis, I can download a program. I guess this how you can do it. And do I have to have somebody else through the hypnosis on me. You know, here is the fun part, the vibration Theta is a low vibration; below consciousness which is Alpha; and a higher vibration and Alphas Beta, which is like schoolroom studying, work mind to work consciousness; and so there is a higher vibration the Beta, the next one down more calm as Alpha. When you go down below the Alpha, Theta which is the hypnosis, or imagination phase as well, because children are in that Theta period for the first seven years mix real world and the imaginary world seamlessly, and that's because Theta is imagination and reality mixed. And then below Theta, there is one lower vibration called Delta, which is absolute sleep. What is significant here? Every day you wake up, you are coming from Delta, the lowest vibration just as you are waking up in the morning, just as you are coming out of sleep immediately like a groggy period, not beginning that's Theta. That's where imagination and hypnosis and reality start to mix together. So guess what? Every day when you are going the bed or when you are waking up, you go through a zone of Theta naturally from sleep vibration, Delta, the lowest, waking up you have to go through Theta. Theta is the imagination so if you put your earphones on and play a program as you are going to bed. Just as your conscious mind lets go and it is not paying attention to the program at this point, you really going off into sleep. Theta is engaged and what is that state doing? Taking the program and downloading it into the subconscious mind because that is what Theta does. Hypnosis, bypassing the conscious mind which just went to sleep, so every night putting earphones on and playing a program of the behavior that you want to create in your life, repetition of that every night, will manifest that experience. So, the first seven years is hypnosis, Theta, auto hypnosis with your earphones and going to bed. That's the first way you can program it.

Number two, the second way is what about programming after age seven. So the conscious mind is working after this age. How do I put a new program, and I say you practice it, you repeat something over and over again, and making a habit out of it as a part of your physical reality. Let's say you want to learn the ABCs, how many times you just start with ABC, and you get to a certain point, and then stop because you did not know what was next, and then you thought about what was next: ABCD and E, and F and you keep adding and, what are you doing, repeating, adding, repeating, adding, and finally you get ABCD... XYZ. And guess what? You got to end and you do not have to do it anymore. Why have you repeated it? Because you made a habit out of it. Now, it is enclosed in the habit mind. You can just call it up. It is already a habit. So repetition, you find that behaviors are not supporting you, then generate a behavior that represents supporting you, and repeat it just like a player on our sporting team. Go out, do the practice, just repeat and repeat it and repeat it again, even if it is not real at that time, it will become real as it becomes downloaded as a program. Your subconscious will download the program, then use it to it and manifest life from it.

So you start out and you may be sick with cancer and your program is, "I am healthy, I control my health," a couple of programs like that is a very positive thing you like that and I stay well. It happens well. It is very hard for your conscious mind to say I am healthy, knowing you have cancer right now. And I say no that is not the issue. You are repeating it, over and over again for what the subconscious, the repetition, habituation occurs in the subconscious, now get the program, what is the program; I am healthy, a function of the mind is to create coherence between your programs and your reality. So if I put in a program that I am healthy and at that moment I am sick with cancer, what do you think the function of my mind is? It is to create an environmental situation where health can be restored. Why? Because my program says I am healthy, my biology is says I am not. The function of the mind is to adjust the biology so it manifests the expression of the program. I can heal myself. But now, with my conscious mind that's good positive thinking. I can heal my inner child, my subconscious. And tell me how much of the day are you using that positive thinking? Less than 5 percent. Oh, it is not going to have so much effect, you want to have an effect put in the subconscious, make a program and operate at 95 percent of the day, so the two fundamental ways right now of learning are the fundamental ways that we acquired the subconscious programs.

A hypnosis in the first seven years has to be repetition of a practice or pattern which occurs after age 7-9. How did you drive a car? You did not know how to drive it when you first got in. You practiced and you experienced all of the aspects of driving, so now you get in the car, you have been driving for a while, you do not even think of the mechanics of the driving part. You put the key in the ignition; you are already thinking about where you are going in a destination. All of this now is automatic subconscious programming and you can turn any aspect of life into that automatic subconscious program. Being in love can be a subconscious program. I say why it is relevant? Well, whether you are just stopping consciously, say, "God, I am so happy and I am in love with this man or just walking down the street I am in love," because that's what my subconscious mind knows as past programming experience in a familiar situation around this aspect. I believe that most of us, and I have seen due to our core beliefs, 80 to 90 percent of people do not love themselves, no self-love. How that can be? And the answer simple, in the previous chapters I also pointed this out. What are the programs in that child's mind (inner child) for the first 7-9 years. And 70 percent of people are redundant, disempowering, so negative and self-sabotaging. How do they get there? Here is the primary reason? Parents act like coaches. I said, what is a coach? Here is the team player. It is not performing growth. It is not putting out the effort and so the coach goes, "You do not deserve to be on this team. Who do you think you are? You are not that good." Why is the coach saying that just to piss off the player? Now, the player now is thinking, "Oh my god, I got to perform better, I am going to work harder. I am going to be better because I want to show the coach that I am deserving of this." So the consciousness of the player, understanding what the coach meant because the coach said you are not good enough, and the consciousness has an interpretation, "I am not good enough because I am not performing well, therefore, I will perform well, but that one student or whoever it is conscious, I said, what about the child before seven? They are not conscious. They are recording, if parent is acting like a coach, what the child just records is: not good enough, not deserving, who do you think you are, you are not that good at this, you are not lovable. These are things parents say. Why do they say them? Because they wanted to be a coach, they are not conscious of what they are doing. They have learned and are programmed like that in their childhood and in their growing environments. There is no blaming anyone here, it is all about being conscious about this information. Because the parent thinks you could do better, it only works if the child is conscious enough to understand the meaning. If the child is under seven, they are just recording the words. What are the words that are recorded in this child's mind; not good enough, not deserving, not lovable, not worthy. These are the some programmed in our subconscious mind. What happened if that mind plays 95 percent the time? What is the function of the mind? To take the program sand create behavior out of it and that will, you know, make coherence between the resulting life and the program. That is not good enough, not worthy, not deserving, then guess what? The behavior is going to come from the mind. Any behavior that will show outside people that I am not good enough, not worthy, not deserving because my behavior will be coherent with the program, and this is why between 80 to 90 percent of the people in our world will not test positive for do I love myself. Because the fundamental programs are critical, self-critical, and why that is a relevant program. I am not lovable, then the issue is when a partner shows up who says they love you, what is your mind thinking at that moment is your subconscious mind can say that what will you do? You will push away love because you cannot accept for yourself so when someone else says that it cannot be true, and therefore you will always will be seeking love and never find it. The conscious mind wishes and desires, yes, I want that but just 5 percent of the day and 95 percent of the time you are not worthy. You do not deserve this, who do you think you are and all the this suddenly be clear, if that's one in the 95 percent of the time, I will never be successful and that is why I am worried about it. And the answer is because that 95 percent of the day not visible to me, so I am sabotaging myself 95 percent of the day with programs that will push away everyone who loves me, and at the end of the day come home and say I cannot find a mate. No one loves me. This did not start there. It started with you. If you do not love you. No one else can love you. Love yourself unconditionally with compassion and radical forgiveness.

CHAPTER FIFTEEN

THE POWER OF FAITH FILLED WITH WORDS: INNER CHILD SELF LOVE AFFIRMATIONS

"Better than a thousand hollow words, is one word that brings peace."

- Buddha

In this chapter, I am offering self-love inner child affirmations. I suggest to you now to choose the affirmations in these pages that you love and write them on paper and record with your own voice and listen while you sleep or before sleep or as soon as you wake up or all day long as much as you have time. As often as possible, listen to them to make it your daily habit, listening to your affirmations with your own voice. It is easy to record and listen on your phone, I suggest using earphones as well. This exercise will help you to elevate and create brain cells and penetrate your subconscious mind, and you will program your mind and create the life, recreate the person you want to be.

Another exercise related to self-love affirmations is powerful mirror work; it is so important to love yourself. Mirror work can help you build the most important relationship of your life: your relationship with yourself. You may think it is so easy and or silly. All those exercises I suggest that you do for at least 21 days. It may, at first, appear too simple to make a difference. What I have learned is persistence is really important here. There is no big or small thing till when you relate with it. But I have learned that the simplest acts are often the most important ones. Small changes in your thinking can lead to huge changes in your live.

Sometimes, it can be challenging to stand in front of the mirror and say to yourself, "I love you," so due to these challenges, I will suggest you go with the flow and keep a journal for yourself. Write down your thoughts and feelings so you can see how you are progressing.

You can try something like this:

- Stand or sit in front of mirror or hold a mirror with your hand.
- Look deep into your eyes.
- Take a breath and repeat the affirmations, such as: I want to like you. I want to learn to love you. Let's go for it and have some fun.
- Take another breath and repeat the affirmation, such as: I am learning to really like you. I am learning to really love you.
- This is the first exercise for you maybe, and I know it can be little uncomfortable, but please stay with it. Keep taking deep breaths. Look into your eyes, see yourself in your eyes, repeat the same affirmation to each eye at least seven times. And use your name as you say: I am willing to love you (name). I am willing to learn to love you.

- Throughout the day, each time you pass a mirror ◌ reflection, please repeat these affirmations, even if have to do it silently.

Being compassionate with yourself provides the care, tenderness and kindness you deserve. Here are some suggestions for providing yourself that consideration:

- Accepting yourself who you are: Everyone has times when they made mistakes or they tried to measure up to what they wanted. If you do make mistakes, accept them without judging yourself; instead, learn from them and aim to do better next time. When you realize that you are just like everybody else in the world. You can calm down and be more at ease.
- Change your voice: say to yourself, "it will be okay, I am okay," instead of continually criticizing yourself, use a calm and gentle voice to replace those thoughts. You can say, "not helpful" or "I did the best I could," as soon as you realize your inner child, inner critic, is attacking you. Repeat these replacements with many times so the new sentiments sink in. Even if this voice as I told before it may not sound originally genuine, keep doing it. Gradually, this new voice will become sincere and you will make the unfamiliar one familiar to yourself.
- Be your best friend: Treat yourself the way you would treat someone you are close to if they feel unloved or unworthy. You can give yourself a big hug and gently rock your body, connect with your body and organs, speak to them. This can soothe you and make you feel cared for and nurtured.
- Think about something that makes you happy: Put your attention on your loved ones; it can be a pet, a child, a

- I am protected by celestial beings of light and love.
- I am here to learn, experience and grow and always remember that it is okay to make mistakes while learning that is the part of learning process of the soul.
- I will experience some tough times, little ones, but remember that those times will always pass and you will grow stronger and wiser every time because you choose to learn. I am the master student and master teacher.
- I have knowingly chosen your body, my parents and place I was born because the higher goods of my learning experience is here on earth.
- The Universe loves you, I love you, You are more than good enough.
- I have always been good enough.
- It is enough to be me.
- I will say or do things in my life or not say things or not do things that will make me question if I am good enough be willing to realize that I am always good enough no matter what.
- I am here to remember I am loved, that I am compassion, I am peace, I am pure universal life force.
- I approve of myself, accept myself, I accept me, accept myself.
- My most important job in this life is to accept life and to accept myself.
- I am part of something much bigger than myself.
- Life is energy and I am a master of energy.

- I realize that I am the one, and the way to master life is to take responsibility for my vibrations.
- I have free will to choose my beliefs, my emotions and actions, I am that powerful, I love myself always, thank you.
- I am unique, I am here to be me, to shine my light.
- I am the divine creator, I may have forgotten that. That is perfectly okay. I choose now to reconnect. I choose now to remember I am universal indulgence.
- It is safe speak my truth, it is safe to be me, it is safe to live my mission.
- It is safe to take care of myself, always follow my intuition.
- I am important to this planet, I am awesome.
- My soul shines through my heart.
- I accept who I am, I am beautiful.
- I am harmonious being.
- Acceptance brings me peace, I accept me.
- My heart is my path to joy, I follow my heart.
- Unconditional love flows through my veins.
- Unconditional love flows through my body.
- Unconditional love flows through my heart.
- I am valuable, I deserve love, and I am loved.
- I am worthy, I am safe, I am loved.

- I approve of myself, I accept myself, I love and forgive myself.
- I am vibration, I am energy vibrating frequencies love, gratitude and happiness.
- I am lovable, I am worth loving.
- I am beautiful, I am joy, I am bliss.
- I am good enough, I am worthy.
- I am magnificent, I love myself.
- I am an energetic being in a human body.
- I love who I am.
- I was born worthy of love.
- I am divine expression of the infinite, the infinite is love, and this is also means I am love.
- I am just wonderful the way I am.
- I am beautiful just the way I am.
- I am a remarkable human being.
- I am smart enough.
- I am strong enough.
- I am enough.
- I am worthy of happiness, joy and bliss.
- I appreciate myself.
- I am unique, I am perfectly different.
- I am a treasure, a gift.

- I am here to be given.
- I am one-of-a-kind.
- I am also one with everything and everyone.
- I am a part of everything, eternal beauty and harmony.
- Just being me is meaningful, I am significant.
- I am important.
- I have meaning and purpose being here.
- I can fill myself with love and let it flow to others.
- Loving myself means I am secure and safe with myself.
- I have a gentle loving heart.
- I have a deep sense of compassion for myself and others.
- I am compassionate, kind, and grateful.
- I am strong when I need to be.
- I am soft when I need to be.
- I am everything within me.
- There is no need to search, I have found myself.
- I am brilliant.
- I am courageous and kind.
- I am intuitive and sensitive.
- I am glorious and gorgeous.
- I have flow within me.
- I have energy within me.

- I have love within me.
- I have compassion within me.
- I have peace within me.
- I have health within me.
- I have wellbeing within me.
- I have worthiness within me.
- I deserve an extraordinary life.
- I am full of joy, fun and peace.
- I deserve to be treated with love and respect.
- I am loving and respectful.
- I am joyful, joy lives within me.
- I am fun, laughter live within me.
- I am love, loves lives within me.
- I respect myself.
- I threat myself love and kindness.
- I can look after myself.
- I can give myself what I need.
- I forgive myself for all my preconceived ideas and limitations.
- I forgive myself for all past times where I have not fully love myself.
- I do not have to be perfect to be lovable.
- I am enormously loving and kind towards myself.

- I am worth loving.
- I deserve to give myself the gift of total acceptance.
- I am attractive.
- I am a sparkling gem.
- I am valuable gift.
- I am shining light.
- I am treasure to behold.
- I have loving thought towards myself.
- I have loving thought towards others.
- I accept myself.
- I love and appreciate my body.
- I love and appreciate my skin.
- I love and appreciate all my organs and muscles.
- I love and appreciate my bones.
- I love and appreciate my eyes, nose and mouth.
- I love and appreciate my arm and legs.
- I love and appreciate every single cell in my body.
- I love and appreciate my brain, mind and intelligence.
- I love an appreciate my creativity.
- I love and appreciate my communication and focus.
- I love and appreciate my attention.
- I love and appreciate my receiving mode.
- I love and appreciate my feel feeling open and receiving.

- I love and appreciate my feelings of acceptance.
- I love and appreciate my kindness to give myself and to others
- I love and appreciate my blossoming consciousness.
- I love and appreciate my abilities.
- I love and appreciate my understanding.
- I love and appreciate all true moment in myself.
- I love and appreciate my memory.
- I love and appreciate all moments of inner peace and calm within me.
- I love and appreciate all who I am.
- I am here therefore, I am worthy.
- I am worthy of goodness in life.
- I am worthy of fun.
- I am worthy of love.
- I am worthy of joy.
- I am worthy of feeling passion and purpose.
- I am worthy of feeling whole and complete.
- I am worthy of feeling solid within myself.
- I am worthy of feeling safe and secure.
- I am worthy of harmonious relationships.
- I am worthy of fulfilling work.
- I am worthy of great health and energy.

- I am worthy of growth and development.
- I feel good about myself.
- I am a happy being who I am.
- I am calm and realized.
- Every day my trust in myself increases.
- I expect good things to happen in my life.
- My imagination now creates whatever I believe and conceive.
- I now have all the resources I need to achieve my goals easily and effortlessly.
- Every day in every way I'm getting better and better.
- I set definite goals and create new Power Affirmations™ to achieve them quickly and easily.
- Today, I am using 100% of my mind's capacity.
- I now have easy access to the information in my subconscious mind.
- All subconscious information is being revealed to me now.
- What I imagine I can do, I can do.
- I receive wisdom and knowledge from God in every moment of my life.
- I am now making amazing progress towards all of my goals.

- My subconscious mind is now revealing everything I need to know to create and fulfill my mission and purpose in life.
- I am consciously aware of my beliefs. I only hold onto beliefs that support me.
- I now see and feel my goals as already accomplished.
- I expand the powers of my subconscious mind every day.
- Whatever I conceive and believe, I can achieve.
- I create my own luck every day.
- I now achieve my goals with joy and laughter.
- I visualize what I want to be and act as if I am already what I visualize.
- Through consistently repeating my Power Affirmations™, I can now create any reality that I desire.
- I am now creating habitual thought patterns of success, positive thinking, and positive living.
- I am now giving me massive momentum towards the specific results I desire.
- I am guided and excited. All I need is within me now.
- I am now filled with faith, certainty, and confidence. I now feel these emotions in my body.
- I am now confident and assertive.
- I now walk and move with assurance, poise, and personal power.
- I am now a powerful and charismatic personality.

- I am growing more and more attractive every day.
- My confidence and competence are exploding massively every day.
- I am now friendly, outgoing, and confident.
- I am now bold and courageous. I now seize my opportunities immediately.
- I now have the ability to change anything in my life that I choose to change. I take complete responsibility for my life.
- When I speak to others, I look them straight in the eye and speak with confidence knowing that I am equal to every person I meet regardless of their social status or accomplishments.
- I can now create a state of total certainty and confidence at a moment's notice anytime I need it.
- I now move my body with poise and confidence.
- Every time I close my eyes and breathe deeply, my confidence expands and fills my whole being.
- I now see myself as exactly the person I want to be: confident, self- assured, healthy, and prosperous.
- I now hold myself and other people in high esteem.
- Every day in every way I am growing more and more confident.
- My confident energy, enthusiasm, and passion are increasing massively every day. Because I am committed to constant and never-ending improvement, my performance is improving every day.

- What I imagine I can do, I can do.
- I am now fearless, courageous and bold.
- I receive wisdom and knowledge from my subconscious mind every moment of my life.
- I apply my faith with consistent acts of courage.
- The expression on my face now communicates certainty and confidence.
- I am now a highly charismatic and powerful person.
- I now inspire and expand my imagination with enthusiasm.
- I now relive the most joyous moments of my life. And these moments inspire me to greater confidence and a greater feeling of self-worth.
- I immerse myself in a powerful environment on a regular basis.
- I act as if I already have all the confidence I need and desire.
- I speak to myself and others with confidence, certainty, and conviction.
- I now take complete and total control of my internal images, dialog, and feelings.
- My subconscious mind now communicates confidence, certainty, and power to the subconscious minds of others.
- My thoughts, presence, charm, and charisma now inspire others to greater self-confidence and personal power.

- I now radiate confidence and certainty in the presence of other people.
- When I speak, the tone of my voice communicates strength, courage, and confidence.
- I am now confident, assertive, and decisive in every situation.
- I now create outstanding confidence by repeatedly rehearsing in my mind and imagining the results I want in advance.
- I am now an outstanding leader who leads with confidence.
- I increase my self-confidence by increasing my skills and abilities every day.
- As I rehearse the results, I want in my thoughts before they happen, my skill and confidence expand massively.
- Other people find me to be a fascinating and interesting person.
- I consciously choose the emotional state that I am in at all times.
- I am now raising my standards in all the major areas of my life and I am holding myself to those standards at all times.
- I now control the pictures, sounds, and feelings that I create in my mind.
- I am now comfortable with a high level of uncertainty in my life knowing that without great risks there are no great rewards.

- I now face challenging situations of great uncertainty with a feeling of absolute certainty and confidence that I can transform any challenge or set back to my advantage.
- I am now positively adventurous and outrageous.
- I now put myself into new positively challenging situations every day.
- I now set new and higher standards for myself and I step up to every challenge in a state of absolute certainty and unstoppable confidence.
- I now put my body into a peak state of absolute certainty knowing that I can create any positive result that I am committed to.
- I am now living a life of design rather than a life of reaction.
- I am now absolutely clear about the specific results I want in every area of my life.
- I now step up with total power and passion to take whatever positive action is necessary to achieve my desired results.
- I now make my future my present. My future is now.
- I now celebrate the achievement of my goals before they occur in the physical world.
- Whenever I set a definite goal, I take immediate action towards its attainment to create and sustain massive momentum.
- I am now spending my time, energy, and emotion on the goals that are most important to me rather than

responding to the demands of other people. I am in control.

- Urgency is not my friend. Through results-focused planning and delegating to others, I minimize the amount of time I spend addressing the urgent demands of other people.
- I now do only what I do best and get other people to do the rest.
- I now delegate tasks that do not require my direct attention and focus to other people.
- My subconscious mind now provides me with the specific massive action plans I need to attain my desired results.
- My subconscious mind is now consistently presenting me with updated plans to achieve my goals even when I am playing, eating, or sleeping.
- I now carefully measure and manage my progress towards my desired results every day.
- I am now highly flexible. I carefully monitor the results that I am getting and quickly adjust my actions until I receive the specific results I desire.
- I accelerate my progress towards my desired results by studying other people who have been outstanding in that area.
- I increase my hunger and desire to achieve my goals every day.
- Using tapes, books, music, and anything else around me that is easily accessible, I now create a controlled

environment that keeps my mind focused on my primary outcomes every day.

- I do not adapt to my environment. I persist in making my environment adapt to me.
- All of my internal images, dialog and feelings are now pulling me towards the results I desire. I am totally committed and congruent.
- I am now focused on the results I want, driven by a passionate purpose, and charted with massive action plans.
- I now see things exactly the way they are, exactly the way I want them, and now take massive action to close that gap.
- I now prepare a results-oriented daily plan every evening for the following day.
- When I reach a definite decision, I commit and resolve to the achievement of the end result I desire.
- I now create magic moments for myself, my family and friends.
- I now celebrate my achievements in advance.

AFTERWORD

I am so happy, dear pure beautiful soul, to have been able to share with you the experience of how to battle with the inner child, which has been so valuable to me in my life, my spiritual journey. My hope is that you, too, will find some wisdom, and it will be valuable in your journey as positive growth and self-care.

In closing, I would love to leave you with 19 ways to you can love yourself now-and always. Let them serve as reminders of what you have learned from reading this book and provide you with ongoing support for a joyful and fulfilling life.

And always, remember and never forget; I love you !

REYHAN TOPLU

19 WAYS YOU CAN LOVE YOURSELF NOW–AND ALWAYS

1. Stop All Criticism.

Criticism never changes things in our lives. Refuse to criticize yourself. Accept yourself exactly as you are.

2. Forgive Yourself.

Let the past go. You did the best you could at the time, with understanding, awareness and knowledge that you had. Now, you are growing and changing, and you will live life differently.

3. Do Not Scare Yourself.

Stop terrorizing yourself with your thoughts. It is a dreadful way to live. Find a mental image that gives you pleasure and immediately switch a scary thought to a pleasant one.

4. Be Gentle And Kind And Patient.

Be gentle with yourself. Be kind to yourself. Be patient with yourself as you learn new ways of thinking. Treat yourself as you would treat anyone you really love.

5. Be Kind To Your Mind.

Self-hatred is hating your own thoughts. Do not hate yourself for having these thoughts. Gently change the thoughts to more life-affirming ones.

6. Praise Yourself.

Criticism breaks down your inner spirit. Praise builds it up. Praise yourself as much as you can. Tell yourself how well you are doing with every little thing.

7. Support Yourself.

Find ways to support yourself. Reach out to friends and allow them to help you. It is being strong to ask for help when you need it.

8. Be Loving To Your Negatives.

Acknowledge that you created them to fulfill a need. Now you are finding new, positive ways to fulfill those needs. Lovingly release the old, negative patterns.

9. Take Care Of Your Body.

Learn about nutrition. What kind of fuel does your body need in order to have optimum energy and vitality? Learn about experience. What kind of exercise do you enjoy? Cherish and revere the temple you live in. Your body, your temple, look after it well with nurturing, care and love.

10. Have Fun!

Remember the things that gave you joy as a child and incorporate them into your life now. Find a way to have fun with everything you do. Let yourself express the joy of living. Smile, laugh, rejoice, and the universe rejoices with you!

11. Love Yourself-Do It Now.

Do not wait until you get well or lose weight or get a new job or find a new relationship. Begin loving yourself now-and do the best you can.

12. Do Your Mirror Work.

Look into your eyes often. Express the growing sense of love you have for yourself. Forgive yourself while looking in the mirror. Talk to your parents while looking in the mirror. Forgive them, too. At least, once.

13. Record Your Voice Audio Self-Love Sleep Affirmations.

Select the self-love affirmation for yourself from previous chapters in order to create yourself and your reality, affirm and record with your own voice, then listen while you sleep. If you have time, listen often as a daily habit.

14. Balancing Your Chakras

Settle yourself in for a chakra balancing guide meditation or listening to chakra-related solfeggio frequencies, go to yoga class, wear the color of the chakra you want to balance, or work with the crystal of the chakras.

15. Healing Body, Mind, Spirit: Yoga

Did you know that many yoga poses balance certain chakras? The Downward Dog is powerful for the base chakra, as three pose (grounding, grounding, grounding!). The Dancer pose opens the heart chakra and strengthens the solar plexus chakra, and simple twists with your chin tucked in and eyes gazing upwards, squeeze the thyroid and it can cleanse the throat chakra, and on and on we could go. Your daily or weekly yoga practice is working to clear, balance and strengthen your chakras, your energy body.

16. Using Crystals

Crystal healing is based on the idea that energetic vibrations from crystals can balance the natural vibration in our bodies to make us feel certain ways. Rose quartz is said to open our hearts to love and as a crystal healer I can claim amethyst brings calming sensations into our daily experiences. There are millions of minerals, crystals and stones outside; you can use them according to your chakra in order to bring harmony and balance into your body, mind and spirit.

17. Journaling, Writing.

In order to cultivate self-love and heal your inner child, journaling really is such a powerful tool. There is no specific format to cultivating self-love or healing with journaling. You can write a love letter to yourself, list all those traits you do not feel comfortable with, and then add, "... but I love myself anyway".

And you can create yourself affirmations and life script and daily write them down till you are emotionally physically, mentally and spiritually aligned with those affirmations. You can always ask questions at the beginning of the day, how you can protect your energy and wellbeing? And the end of the day, ask how you feel and progress. If you love yourself unconditionally with flow, know and treat yourself how you want to be treated. It will change your entire life and perception as it changed my life and many others.

18. Essential Oils.

Essential oils through the ancient times have been used to harness the healing power of growing things on the earth. Flowers and shrubs, trees, roots and bark. There are many essential oils today in order to cure, balance dozens of health issues. They have the ability to clean our homes and our bodies without using toxic chemicals. I honestly use them every day in my life in an oil diffuser with many different essential oils. They help to elevate your mood, so whenever you are having a challenging day or want to change or lift your energy, you can use them accordingly. Each essential oil represents and is connected to our chakras. Orange, mint, jasmine, sandalwood, and lavender are the most common I am using for myself. Some brands come up with essential oil for each chakras; each oil balance a related chakra. You know about chakras such as sacral chakra is represented by the orange color, so you can use orange essence oil for balancing that chakra.

19. Meditation.

I am a big advocate of meditation. Meditation is for me is a form of mindfulness. It is turning the concentration, the consciousness, inward and reaching relaxed states. Now, there are many avenues within you can do it through breathing, through contemplation of an object, through chanting, these all different forms of meditation. I use breathing to focus my breath and mindfulness. It is being aware without thoughts without distractions, just aware of what's going on at the present moment at all levels physically, mentally, emotionally, and spiritually. And all of these are incredibly recuperative to meditate. You clean the decks, you get rid of anxiety, all the stress hormones and chemicals that have built up, this dissipates, because you are in this calm, conscious, mindful state. It is very, very beneficial and helps me grow and evolve along my journey as part of my daily routine. It will help and elevate you as well. Just try it.

NOTES

Chapter 4

Damasio, Antonio R.. "Descartes' error: emotion, reason, and the human brain. avon books." (1994).

Narvaez, Darcia & Gray, Peter & McKenna, James & Fuentes, Agustin & Valentino, Kristin. (2014). Children's Development in Light of Evolution and Culture. 10.1093/acprof:oso/9780199964253.003.0001.

Chapter 5

Minullina, A. (2018)Psychological Trauma Of Children Of Dysfunctional Families.65-74. 10.15405/epsbs.2018.09.8.

Chapter 8

Hanh,Thich Nhat,Reconciliation: Healing the Inner Child.. Parallax Press, Oct 9, 2006 31-32

Chapter 11

Wallace D Wattles,The Science Of Getting Rich (1910),15.

ABOUT THE AUTHOR

Reyhan Toplu is an holistic healing and mindfulness practitioner, scholar, yogini, and author who offers her blending lifetime skills and knowledge with holistic; body mind spirit approach. Reyhan focuses on the multidimensional needs of individual. Recognizing a need for greater spiritual awareness in society, Reyhan has devoted her life on especially inner child healing, self-love, teaching mindfulness and helping people in all age groups who need to discover and develop their creative power of self-healing and personal growth. She also has integrated her accredited yoga, meditation, reiki, shamanic healing and other healing practices into her private healing & therapy work and public course offerings. And she is also writing her next book "Mindful Compassion for Suffering". Meet Reyhan and get ready to discover more joy, bliss and harmony in your life at: www.reyhantoplu.com.

Thank you!

Get Your Free Mandala Coloring Book! Please Visit My Website.

www.reyhantoplu.com

Printed in Great Britain
by Amazon

54534800R00139